A Policy for Peace

A Policy for Peace

Field Marshal
Lord Carver

faber and faber

First published in 1982 by
Faber and Faber Limited
3 Queen Square London WC1N 3AU
Printed in Great Britain by
Redwood Burn, Trowbridge, Wiltshire

Library of Congress Cataloging in Publication Data

Carver, Michael, 1915–
A policy for peace.

Includes index.
1. Atomic weapons and disarmament. I. Title.
JX1974.7.C35 1982 327.1′74 82–11684
ISBN 0–571–11975–1 AACR2

British Library Cataloguing in Publication Data
Carver, Michael
A policy for peace.
1. Military policy
I. Title
355′.0335 UA1
ISBN 0–571–11969–7 (cased)
0–571–11975–1 (pbk)

Contents

Preface

In the last three years I have found myself engaged in public discussion of the renewed controversy over nuclear weapons. My involvement in this arose from two events: first, I was created a life peer, with the concomitant responsibility for contributing to discussion of defence matters in the House of Lords: secondly, as an ex-Chief of the Defence Staff and in response to a request, I wrote a very brief letter to the Defence and External Affairs Sub-Committee of the Expenditure Committee of the House of Commons in December 1978, when it was examining the future of the United Kingdom's nuclear weapon policy. The Committee's report was overtaken by the change of administration following the General Election in May 1979 and was published, incomplete, in April of that year. My letter, printed as Appendix 3, was noticed by the producer of a BBC television programme on the issue of the replacement of the Polaris submarine force. He thought it unlike what he would have expected from an ex-Chief of the Defence Staff, and an interview with me on the subject was included in the programme.

As a result partly of that and partly of a speech I had made in the House of Lords, I was, and continue to be, invited to take part in discussions and debates and to give lectures and talks, principally in universities and schools, not only on the narrower issue of whether or not the British independent strategic deterrent force should be maintained—and, if so, how—but also on the whole issue of nuclear weapons and nuclear deterrent strategy. I was not surprised to discover that most people, whatever their age, nationality or profession, find the subject so complicated and abstruse that they tend to swing to one or other of the extremes: support for the total abolition of nuclear weapons or conviction that we (either Britain or the West as a whole) must have at least as many as the Soviet Union, type for type, or preferably more.

Having initially been rather reluctant to enter the arena, I have felt impelled to do so in order to try to persuade those responsible for deciding these matters, and those whose opinions influence them, that both these extreme views are misguided and could be disastrous and that there is another policy that could preserve peace and reduce the likelihood that mankind will be subjected to the horrors of a nuclear war.

I therefore welcomed the invitation by Faber and Faber to write a short book on the subject in order to reach a wider public, to be able to set out more fully the reasoning that has led to my holding the views that I do and also to clarify my own position, which I have found is apt to be misrepresented. My attitude is not based, as some suggest, merely on a wish that the army should receive a larger share of the defence budget but results from a study of the subject that originated many years ago. My views crystallized in the years 1957–9, when I was a student at the Imperial Defence College (now the Royal College of Defence Studies) and then Director of Plans at the War Office. At that time I was engaged in almost continuous correspondence and discussion about a wide variety of military subjects, some historical, some current, with Basil Liddell Hart, who was developing his own attitude to nuclear weapons, set out in his book *Deterrent or Defence*, published in 1960. We had first exchanged views, principally on armoured warfare, in the early 1950s, when I was working for Field Marshal Montgomery at NATO's Supreme Headquarters Allied

Powers Europe. I was then head of his exercise planning staff, one of the principal subjects considered in his annual study periods being the possible use of nuclear weapons in support of the land battle. In developing these exercises, I had frequent discussions with André Beaufre, then head of NATO's Interallied Tactical Study Group. The contribution that Liddell Hart and Beaufre (who were close friends) made to the development of thought on the subject was as notable as it has been neglected.

As will become evident to the reader, my principal criticism of NATO's, including Britain's, nuclear deterrent policy is that it remains a hang-over from the days of American monopoly and predominance, which ended over twenty years ago. As in so many military matters, the established dogma becomes set in concrete by the vested interests it creates and the great mental and material problems raised by changing it. Short of trying it out—which nobody in their senses would wish to do—there is no proof that one idea is better than another. One can only fall back on reason and logic, and one has to admit that at the heart of nuclear deterrent strategy there lies a paradox that is not susceptible to a logical solution.

In the pages that follow I hope to persuade the reader that all that the huge nuclear arsenals in the hands of the rival giant powers now do is to deter them both from going to war with each other and, if that measure were tragically to fail, to deter them from using nuclear weapons—a twofold influence that makes a notable contribution to world peace; that their deterrent value cannot be extended to cover other situations; that the number and variety of their weapons systems is grossly in excess of what is needed to provide that deterrence; and that additional independent systems are superfluous. I have been encouraged in making my views known to the public by the support of a number of very distinguished experts in this field, among whom, in Britain, I would cite Professors Michael Howard, Lord Zuckerman and Lawrence Freedman, as well as many in the United

States of America. The latter include, notably, the authors of a highly significant article entitled 'Nuclear Weapons and the Atlantic Alliance', published in the spring 1982 issue of the journal *Foreign Affairs*—McGeorge Bundy, George F. Kennan, Robert S. McNamara and Gerard Smith. Strengthened by the support of these highly intelligent and experienced men, I can face with equanimity the criticism, frequently levelled at me by Ministers of the Government, that I am the only living British ex-Chief of the Defence Staff to hold the views I do. Throughout my military service, I have been accustomed to being out of step.

April 1982

1

Absolute War

War is the final resort in the struggle for power. Civil wars are concerned with the struggle for power within nation-states. International wars, wars between nation-states, are concerned either with extending or maintaining the power that a nation exercises over other nations, in its own interest, in the world outside its borders or, in some cases, with containing the threat of the absorption of all or part of one nation into another.

Why do nations, groups of people within nations and individuals within those groups wish to exercise power? Partly because power brings influence which can be used for their own material benefit, partly in order that society may be organized according to the ideas that the individual, group or nation favours for one reason or another, partly because, again for various reasons, the individual, group or nation claims or aspires to superiority over others. Generally speaking, all these motives fuse to inspire a strong feeling of cohesion, reinforced by the fear that if one's own group does not assert its claim to power and influence, it will be submerged by another, suffering material, cultural and psychological disadvantage as a result. The struggle for power can therefore be represented as the need to preserve one's own society. The individuals who lead such struggles often genuinely believe that they are doing their best for the sake of their fellow citizens.

This struggle also goes on within nation-states, but unless

it erupts into violence, it is carried on by other means—through the workings of the economy and the process of politics. Its eruption into violence is prevented or contained principally by the conventions of society, by the fact that the majority of the people who comprise a nation generally choose to abide by these conventions and to acquiesce in their reinforcement by the law and its agents, notably the police. The struggle goes on at lower levels, even within the family. Struggle is endemic.

But as within the nation, so between nations contestants generally prefer to achieve their aims without resort to violence, unless they are fanatics who like fighting and violence for their own sake and for the excitement they offer. The normal method of carrying on the struggle is through pressure—economic, cultural and psychological. Through the everyday working of the world economy, through verbal exchanges in many forms and through political contact, a perpetual game is played out in which nation-states compete with each other for resources, for influence and for their several interests, including the preservation of their cultures. Unless they are threatened by drastic deprivation in any of these fields, competition is generally adjusted without resort to violence, although the threat of its use may play a part in persuasion. In previous ages resort to force was much more common than it is today, partly because the consequences of resorting to force were not out of proportion to the causes that were at stake—or so it seemed to those who embarked upon war. The wars of the seventeenth and eighteenth centuries in Europe were of this nature. The armies involved were not large—less than 100,000 on each side; battles were few and far between; operations ceased in the winter; and the direct effect on the life of the countries involved, even including those frequently fought over like the Netherlands, caused no intense hardship. In any case, life was simple in those days.

But Napoleon's wars introduced a new dimension. His mass armies (he led 600,000 men into Russia in 1812), in which artillery was beginning to play a significant part, lived off the country. His conduct of war involved great battles to eliminate the enemy's armed forces, and over twenty years of this sort of war proved a heavy burden for Europe to bear.

After the final battle of Waterloo in 1815, the statesmen of Europe were determined to see that nothing of the same sort happened again, and although Europe was not spared war in that century, they were successful—until 1914. While they were deliberating at Vienna and attempting to establish a stable balance of power in Europe, Karl Maria von Clausewitz, a colonel in the Prussian army who had served both with that army and with the Russians when the Prussians were on Napoleon's side, was turning over in his highly intelligent mind the whole question of the nature of war and how it should be conducted. In 1818 he was promoted to major-general and appointed Director of the War Academy in Berlin. In that capacity he began an exhaustive study of Napoleon's campaigns and set down his conclusions in a massive book, which he had not completed when he died of cholera in 1831. It was published by his widow in 1832 under the title *Vom Kriege* (*On War*). It quickly became, and has remained ever since, the strategist's Bible; and, as with the Bible, quotations can be found in it to suit all tastes and to justify conflicting opinions.

Clausewitz defined war as 'an act of force to compel our enemy to do our will'.[1] His analysis of Napoleon's campaigns led him to the conclusion that success depended on the maximum use of force, and he wrote:

> Kind-hearted people might, of course, think that there was some ingenious way to disarm or defeat an enemy without too much bloodshed, and might imagine this is the true goal of the art of war. Pleasant as it sounds, it is a

---

[1] K. M. von Clausewitz, *On War*, edited and translated by Michael Howard and Peter Paret (Princeton: Princeton University Press, 1976), Book One, ch. I, sect. 2, p. 75.

> fallacy that must be exposed: war is such a dangerous business that the mistakes which come from kindness are the very worst. The maximum use of force is in no way incompatible with the simultaneous use of the intellect. If one side uses force without compunction, undeterred by the bloodshed it involves, while the other side refrains, the first will get the upper hand. That side will force the other to follow suit: each will drive his opponent towards extremes, and the only limiting factors are the counterpoises inherent in war. This is how the matter must be seen. It would be futile—even wrong—to try and shut one's eyes to what war really is from sheer distress at its brutality.[1]

He developed this theme at great length, eventually asserting that one must concentrate all one's efforts in an attempt to destroy the enemy's armed forces: when one had done so, one could impose one's will on him. The means to this end was battle, not the long-drawn-out succession of manoeuvre and siege that had characterized war before Napoleon appeared on the scene.

Seven long books were devoted to the elaboration of this theme and to the issue of how to conduct war on this basis, which he christened Absolute War. But when he turned to the composition of Book Eight, entitled 'War Plans', he had to face the fact that war is meant to have a purpose. Just to impose one's will on the enemy is not enough: there must be some reason why one decides to resort to force in order to impose one's will, some policy behind the act. 'No one starts a war,' he wrote, '—or rather no one in his senses ought to do so—without first being clear in his mind what he intends to achieve by that war and how he intends to conduct it'.[2] This statement led him on to his famous definition, which takes slightly different forms in different places but is most fully explained in Book Eight, chapter 6. It is worth quoting

---

[1] ibid., sect. 3.
[2] ibid., Book Eight, ch. 2, p. 574.

in its context:

> It is, of course, well known that the only source of war is politics—the intercourse of governments and peoples; but it is apt to be assumed that war suspends that intercourse and replaces it by a wholly different condition, ruled by no law but its own.
>
> We maintain, on the contrary, that war is simply a continuation of political intercourse, with the addition of other means. We deliberately use the phrase 'with the addition of other means' because we also want to make it clear that war in itself does not suspend political intercourse or change it into something entirely different. In essentials, that intercourse continues, irrespective of the means it employs. The main lines along which military events progress, and to which they are restricted, are political lines that continue throughout the war into the subsequent peace. How could it be otherwise? Do political relations between peoples and between their governments stop when diplomatic notes are no longer exchanged? Is war not just another expression of their thoughts, another form of speech or writing? Its grammar, indeed, may be its own, but not its logic.
>
> If that is so, then war cannot be divorced from political life; and whenever this occurs in our thinking about war, the many links that connect the two elements are destroyed and we are left with something pointless and devoid of sense.[1]

In other words, war is meant to result in a better state of peace, at least as seen from one's own point of view. Although waging an Absolute War may result in victory and the ability to impose one's will on the enemy, the destruction and damage it causes and the desire for revenge which it provokes may negate the original purpose of going to war: it will have failed to be a 'continuation of political intercourse'. In the following sections of that chapter he

[1] ibid., ch. 6, sect. B, p. 605.

went on to discuss aspects of fighting limited wars, such as the occupation of a portion of the enemy's territory and its subsequent use as a bargaining counter with which to extract the desired concession.

It was unfortunate that Clausewitz died before he could resolve the paradox to which his study had led him, and even more unfortunate that his disciples, including especially the elder Moltke, founder of the Prussian General Staff and architect of Bismarck's victories, concentrated their attention on his theory of Absolute War to the neglect of his final conclusions. They were all the more inclined to do so as technical developments in the nineteenth century made it possible to accentuate the absoluteness of Absolute War. Clausewitz had pointed out that absoluteness would always be modified by what he called the 'friction' of the battlefield—all the factors which militated against the ability to concentrate maximum force and then to employ it. The development of railways to carry the troops and their supplies, and of the telegraph to transmit orders and information and to make executive arrangements, allied to the power of governments to impose compulsory military service on every able-bodied man, meant that large masses of men could be concentrated in one place within a short space of time and kept supplied on arrival. The combination of these factors and improvements in firearms and artillery led to much higher casualties when armies clashed—the American Civil War being an early example. The introduction of the machine-gun and further improvements in artillery took this process further and drove the infantryman to seek shelter in the ground, the Russo–Japanese War (1904–5) bringing this development to the notice of prescient soldiers.

By that time military strength appeared to depend on a combination of railway systems and numbers of men, and it was fear that the 'other side' could gain a decisive temporary advantage that escalated the incident of the murder of the Austrian Archduke Francis Ferdinand on 28 June 1914 into the war that engulfed Europe and 'called in the New World to redress the balance of the Old'. The only state policy of which that war was a 'continuation by other means' was that of maintaining a balance of power in Europe, and it is to the eternal discredit of the European statesmen of that time that they did not treat it as a 'continuation of political intercourse' and make a serious attempt, once the battle-lines had solidified at the end of 1914, to return from 'other means' to the normal methods of political exchange. Instead they encouraged their populations to regard the enemy as beyond the Pale, people with whom it was impossible to come to an agreement. They were following the line that Ferdinand Foch had laid down in *The Principles of War*:

> We find ourselves in the presence of an adversary who has the same idea of fighting, who takes up arms for an idea, a principle, no matter what the end, so that it be a policy to be obtained. Invasion or occupation of territory will therefore trouble him very little: these operations cannot be the end of the war. He intends moreover, as we do, to back his political and financial theories by force. He will only renounce those theories when he has been deprived of the means of defending them. He will only confess himself beaten when he is no longer able to fight: that is, when his army has been materially and morally destroyed. Therefore modern war can consider only those arguments which lead to the destruction of that army: namely battle, overthrow by force.[1]

These principles were far removed from those recommended by the famous Chinese expert on military affairs, Sun Tzu. In about 500 BC he had taught that one should not forget that after a war one had to live peaceably alongside the enemy whom one had been fighting, and that one should aim to achieve victory in the shortest possible time, at the least possible cost in lives and effort and having

---

[1] Translated by Hilaire Belloc (London: Chapman & Hall, 1921).

inflicted on the enemy the fewest possible casualties.

There were many reasons why the opposing sides conducted the war as they did: one of them was certainly a misinterpretation of Clausewitz, which represented him as teaching that once war had been embarked upon, it had to be pursued by the use of all available resources until the enemy's forces were totally defeated, and that state policy became subservient to the needs of that strategy until victory (or defeat) had been achieved. As we have seen, this was the very opposite of his final conclusions. Further on in the chapter from which I have already quoted he wrote:

> We can now see that the assertion that a major military development, or the plan for one, should be a matter for *purely military* opinion is unacceptable and can be damaging. Nor indeed is it sensible to summon soldiers, as many governments do when they are planning a war, and ask them for *purely military advice*. But it makes even less sense for theoreticians to assert that all available military resources should be put at the disposal of the commander so that on their basis he can draw up purely military plans for a war or a campaign. It is in any case a matter of common experience that despite the great variety and development of modern war, its major lines are still laid down by governments; in other words, if we are to be technical about it, by a purely political and not a military body.
>
> This is as it should be. No major proposal required for war can be worked out in ignorance of political factors; and when people talk, as they often do, about harmful political influence on the management of war, they are not really saying what they mean. Their quarrel should be with the policy itself, not with its influence. If the policy is right—that is, successful—any intentional effect it has on the conduct of the war can only be to the good. If it has the opposite effect, the policy itself is wrong.[1]

[1] Clausewitz, *On War*, Book Eight, ch. 6, sect. B, p. 607.

At the end of that long and costly struggle, which, if it was meant to maintain the balance of power in Europe, actually resulted in changing it totally, to the detriment of the whole of the continent, the reaction, like that after the Napoleonic wars, was 'never again'. Absolute War, as absolute as the results of the Industrial Revolution could make it, had frustrated the aims of policy, as Clausewitz had realized. Reaction to it took different forms: isolationism, both in the United States and in Britain; internationalism, the attempt to establish a world order, ending the anarchic relations of sovereign nation-states; pacifism and other movements to reduce or abolish armaments; and a new look at strategy.

Foremost among the exponents of this new look were the British military thinkers J. F. C. Fuller and Basil Liddell Hart. Both were trenchant critics of the tactics and strategy that had been employed on the western front—frontal assaults by infantry after massive artillery bombardments, reliance on the progressive attrition of the enemy's material and human resources to wear him down, victory eventually falling into the hands of those with the greater resources of both. Fuller had been impressed by the success of Ludendorff's counteroffensive in March 1918 in affecting the command organization and morale of Haig's army. He concluded that the true aim of military operations should be not the destruction of the enemy's armed forces, as Clausewitz had taught, but the paralysis of their nerve centres, the command and communications system. The aeroplane and the tank, both of them in their infancy in the closing stages of the war, were the weapons with which to achieve this, by restoring mobility to the battlefield. In his book *The Reformation of War*, published in 1923, Fuller extended this thought to consideration of direct attack against the nation's nerve centres, and wrote:

> I believe that, in future warfare, great cities, such as London, will be attacked from the air, and that a fleet of 500 aeroplanes, each carrying 500 ten-pound bombs of,

> let us suppose, mustard gas, might cause 200,000 minor casualties and throw the whole city into panic within half an hour of their arrival. Picture, if you can, what the result will be: London for several days will be one vast raving Bedlam, the hospitals will be stormed, traffic will cease, the homeless will shriek for help, the city will be in pandemonium. What of the government at Westminster? It will be swept away by an avalanche of terror. Then will the enemy dictate his terms which will be grasped at like a straw by a dying man. Thus may war be won in 48 hours and the losses of the winning side be actually nil.[1]

Liddell Hart echoed this theme two years later in his book *Paris, or the Future of War*, in which he wrote:

> Imagine for a moment that, of two centralized industrial nations at war, one possesses a superior air force, the other a superior army. Provided that the blow be sufficiently swift and powerful, there is no reason why within a few hours, or at most days, from the commencement of hostilities, the nerve system of the country inferior in air power should not be paralysed.[2]

The theme was developed in detail by the Italian airman Giulio Douhet, whose prediction that air power, employed for this purpose, would supersede the influence of sea power was music to the ears of the air forces of the major military nations, struggling to free themselves of the shackles that bound them to the conservative influence of armies and navies. These ideas were a decisive step away from the conventions of war that tried to limit the fighting and its direct effects to the armed forces of the contestants, which had been codified in the Hague Convention of 1907 and supported by the activities of the International Red Cross. On the whole, the conventions had been observed by both sides, although naval blockade was a long-established

---

[1] London: Hutchinson, 1923, p. 150.
[2] London: Kegan Paul, 1925, p. 48.

divergence from them. The supporters of these concepts could claim Clausewitz as their mentor, since they concurred with his definition of the aim of war as the imposition of one's will on the enemy; but their divergence from his conclusions about the subservience of the military aim to policy and political intercourse was further influenced by the tendency of the military on both sides to blame the long delay in achieving victory in one case and defeat in the other on their politicians, who had denied them the resources they demanded, squabbled among each other or interfered with, and frustrated, their military plans. In fact, the politicians should be condemned for the opposite fault, for allowing the military to grind on with their ineffective operations and for taking no initiative in seeking a political solution.

The prophecies of Fuller, Liddell Hart and Douhet about the ability to achieve victory 'at one stroke' by air attacks on cities (probably using gas, although the Geneva Convention of 1925 outlawed its use) were based on a gross exaggeration of the effects of air bombardment, given the capability of air forces not only at the time that they were writing but also at the time of the outbreak of the Second World War in 1939. Indeed, they were not to become realistic until the appearance of the atom bomb in 1945, in spite of the fearful destruction caused by massed aircraft raids on Germany and Japan in the later stages of that war. But the exaggerated fear of air attack, including the use of gas, was a potent factor in encouraging anti-war movements in Europe and in persuading Britain and France to try to meet the demands of Hitler and Mussolini through political concessions rather than 'other means'. Having resorted to 'other means' in 1939, their skill at employing them effectively was revealed to be painfully restricted, Germany having profited from the opportunity to start again from scratch, unburdened by imperial commitments. She was restoring mobility to the battlefield, on the lines favoured by Fuller and Liddell Hart, in addition to their emphasis on direct attack on cities, the combination of the two being described by the latter as the 'strategy of the indirect approach'.

Hitler sought political accommodation after his defeat of France, but the terms were not negotiable with Britain as long as the hope of once more 'calling in the New World to redress the balance of the Old' remained a possibility. In June 1940 Churchill, by nature a gambler, took a chance in judging the balance of military risk and what was at stake. Hitler's attack on the USSR and Japan's on the United States' fleet at Pearl Harbor in 1941 tilted the balance decisively in favour of Churchill's judgement. But once the war had thus been extended into a true world war, the influences at work were forced into the pattern of Absolute War, not only because, as in the 1914–18 war, each side described the other as barbarian, but also because the political aim of those fighting against Germany was the total elimination of a regime that could treat human beings as Hitler's did. The development of the atom bomb (as it was then called) was the ultimate step in the conduct of Absolute War, an extension of the fatal concept of direct attack on cities, no longer inhibited by the 'friction' on which Clausewitz had relied to keep the conduct of Absolute War within bounds and to prevent it from frustrating the achievement of state policy. However, its development owed more to the fear that the Germans would produce one before the Allies did and would only be deterred from using it by the threat of retaliation (as, it was believed, they had been deterred from resort to chemical warfare) than it did to any intention to employ it against German cities. It probably would not have been used against them if it had been available before Germany surrendered, although the threat of its use might well have been employed to induce surrender.

The explosions at Hiroshima and Nagasaki in August 1945 initiated a fundamentally new era in the history of warfare. Although the immediate effects of the explosions were not very different in scale from those of the massive air raids which the British and US air forces had carried out on

German and Japanese cities such as Hamburg, Dresden and Tokyo, the fact that they were caused 'in the twinkling of an eye'[1] and that both the direct and indirect effects on human beings had lasting consequences, including genetic ones, greatly intensified the horror of the events. For some time after, and even in some cases to this day, airmen were inclined to represent the atom bomb as merely a further development of air attack that made no difference to the basic principles on which war should be conducted. The aim was still to paralyse the enemy's will, and this was a super-efficient way of doing it. But at least both those who had suffered and those who had produced and delivered the bombs understood the fundamental significance of the change. Michael Mandelbaum, in his book *The Nuclear Question*,[2] rightly pays tribute to the farsightedness of two Americans concerned with the problem at that time. One was the strategic thinker and writer Bernard Brodie. He recognized that its power was of a fantastically greater order than that of previous weapons; that it existed and could not be wished away; that the possibility of developing an adequate defence against it was very remote; and that other powers, besides Britain and Canada, would acquire the capacity to produce nuclear bombs in quantity within five or ten years (he was writing in 1946). He was way ahead of his time in realizing that the deterrent effect of a nuclear monopoly was not likely to last long, but, in opposition to Robert Oppenheimer, he did not accept that possession of nuclear weapons would necessarily prove to be to the advantage of a power bent on aggression. That would only be the case, he argued, if 'the nation which proposes to launch the attack will not need to fear retaliation: the fact that it destroys its opponent's cities some hours or even days

[1] Thomas Schelling, *Arms and Influence*, quoted by Mandelbaum, *The Nuclear Question*, p. 3.
[2] Cambridge: Cambridge University Press, 1979.

before its own are destroyed may avail it little'.[1] He clearly saw that the safeguard against nuclear attack was the ability to retaliate, the implication being that the retaliatory force must be able to survive the enemy's attack.

The other prescient view was that of the highly conservative American Secretary for the Army, Henry Stimson. Prompted by Oppenheimer, he realized the political significance of the weapon, particularly *vis-à-vis* relations with the Soviet Union. A month after Japan had surrendered he sent a memorandum to President Truman, in which he wrote:

> My idea of an approach to the Soviets would be a direct proposal after discussion with the British that we should be prepared to enter into an arrangement with the Russians, the general purpose of which would be to limit the use of the atomic bomb as an instrument of war, and so far as possible to direct and encourage the development of atomic power for peaceful and humanitarian purposes.[2]

These two prophetic statements unfortunately fell on deaf ears. The United States continued to act on the assumption that her monopoly could be maintained, and the unrealistic proposals for the international control of atomic energy embodied in the Baruch Plan foundered on the predictable opposition of the Soviet Union to a scheme that would not only have left the United States with the knowledge of how to construct nuclear weapons while denying it to the USSR, but would also have involved a derogation of her sovereignty and a restriction of her freedom of action, both of which she had just fought a devastating war to preserve. The Baruch Plan, which

[1] Brodie, *The Absolute Weapon* (New York: Harcourt, Brace, 1946), quoted by Mandelbaum, p. 19.

[2] Henry Stimson and McGeorge Bundy, *On Active Service in Peace and War* (New York: Harper & Row, 1947), p. 645, quoted by Mandelbaum, p. 21.

President Truman proposed to the United Nations Organization in 1946, had its origins in the mind of the Danish physicist Niels Bohr, who had been involved in the scientific aspects of atomic fission. During the war he had tried to persuade both American and British authorities to place atomic energy under international control, but had met with little response, although in September 1944 Vannevar Bush and James Conant, prominent scientists engaged in the development of the first atom bomb, suggested to Stimson that, after the war, the weapons should be placed under international control. Stimson's political instinct was sounder in preferring a restricted political negotiation between those principally concerned, with a limited aim, rather than an all-embracing international agreement. 'Action of any international group of nations,' he wrote after the Potsdam Conference in 1945, 'including many small nations, who have not yet demonstrated their political power or responsibility in this war, would not, in my opinion, be taken seriously by the Soviets.'[1]

He was right. The Baruch Plan proposed that all atomic bombs should be placed under the supervision of an international body that would have the power to 'inflict immediate, swift and sure punishment' on any nation that tried to acquire them. This body, which would be set up under the auspices of the United Nations, would not be subordinate to the Security Council and, therefore, not subject to a veto by one of its permanent members. The Russian counterproposal, tabled by Andrei Gromyko, was for an international convention prohibiting the production and employment of 'weapons based on the use of atomic energy', accompanied by the destruction of all existing weapons within three months of the convention coming into force. Any body set up to monitor the convention and any other aspects of atomic energy must be subject to a veto in

---

[1] ibid.

the Security Council and should only become effective after the United States had destroyed all her weapons. No common ground between the rival proposals, each of which clearly favoured its proposer, had been found when the Soviet Union exploded her first device on 23 September 1949, sealing the end of the pursuit of international control. It is open to doubt whether Stimson's proposal would have overcome the mutual suspicions of both sides, but it would have stood a better chance; and, indeed, negotiations that followed its pattern were to prove more effective, limited though their results were, than the international approach so popular with the 'liberal' fraternity.

2

The Absolute Weapon

For a few more years it was still possible to think of the atom bomb as fundamentally no different from the strategic bombing of the Second World War—similar effects could now be produced with far fewer aircraft. The difficulties and expense of producing a weapon were thought to be such that not even a major industrial nation could afford to own more than a handful, and the Russian threat did not seem too serious to the United States, as the Soviet Union had no strategic long-range air force. Even if she developed one, she would be faced with far more severe problems in attacking targets in America than the US Air Force, with its bases in Europe, would have in attacking the Soviet Union. However, President Truman was dissuaded from using one against the Chinese in Korea, when they drove MacArthur back from the Yalu in December 1950. The representations made to him by the British Prime Minister, Clement Attlee, stressed the political implications of its use once more against an Asian nation, and the fear that the Soviet Union might retaliate in some way against Europe.

The first development that finally made it clear to even the most conservative airman that an entirely new order of weapon had come on the scene was the production of the hydrogen or fusion bomb in 1952. One of these could totally destroy even the largest city, and there appeared to be no theoretical limit to the yield which one could be designed to produce. Up to that point the United States had not instituted any fundamental review of her strategy, assuming that the use of atomic weapons would merely be one of the arrows in the quiver of the US Air Force's strategic air command. But knowledge of the effects that the weapon was likely to produce prompted President Eisenhower to initiate such a review. It was in train when the first fusion bomb was exploded on 1 November 1952, confirming the predictions of its designers. A rival technical path forward had been urged by Oppenheimer, that of smaller fission weapons. Rather than develop indiscriminate weapons of ever greater yields, designed to obliterate cities (a contravention of the conventions of war on a far more massive scale than the two dropped on Japan), he wished to see a return to the idea that fighting should, as far as possible, be confined to the armed forces of the contestants and to targets that had a direct military connection with them. Instead of choosing between the two rival solutions, Eisenhower's administration decided to pursue both.

The strategy that evolved from the study he had ordered was that of massive retaliation, linked to the policy of containment pursued by his Secretary of State, John Foster Dulles. The latter attempted to draw a line across the world, surrounding the Communist bloc (Mao Tse-tung had finally established his authority over the whole of China in 1949), beyond which penetration by Communist forces would be met by massive retaliation on the offending country. Conventional forces, defending the line of containment, would act as a tripwire. NATO was to provide these in Europe, and the line of containment was later to be extended across Asia by the South-East Asia Treaty Organization and, between the two, the Central Treaty Organization, which developed from the British-initiated Baghdad Pact. Eisenhower's Republican administration was inclined to support this policy because of two factors. First was its determination to tolerate no repetition of the Korean War. Never again should the most powerful nation in the world be forced to fight an old-fashioned war of attrition, in which the limitations imposed on it prevented the use of the power it possessed to force a decision. The second factor, linked to this, was the reluctance of the administration to spend money on defence. The massive retaliation-cum-tripwire strategy did not require a large army, and, at that stage, it seemed that a comparatively modest strategic air force could provide all the retaliation needed.

America's allies in NATO, which had been formed as a reaction to events in Czechoslovakia and the Berlin crisis of 1948–9, were equally unwilling to shoulder an even heavier burden than they carried already. Britain had initiated a major rearmament programme in 1950 to meet the needs of European defence; she was contributing to the UN forces in Korea and was saddled with many imperial commitments, as France was also. NATO had established a requirement for ninety divisions to meet the threat posed by the Russian army in Central Europe. There was not the faintest hope of this number being provided, even with the rearmament of West Germany. The United States pressed hard for the latter against the opposition of the French and of other countries that had been occupied by the Germans in the Second World War. After the failure of the plan put forward by the French Prime Minister, René Pleven, to form a European Defence Community with integrated forces, no national unit being greater than a battalion, agreement was finally reached to accept West Germany in 1955 as a full member of NATO. The key to the agreement was the undertaking given by Britain, on the initiative of the Foreign Secretary, Anthony Eden, to maintain a force of four divisions and a tactical air force on the continent.

By 1954 it had become clear that the forces to repel the threat of Communist expansion beyond the containment line were indeed not going to be much more than a tripwire, but, even with the superiority in the nuclear field that the United States then enjoyed, the concept of immediate massive retaliation was not alone considered sufficient to prevent expansion. The alternative technical version to the fusion bomb, namely smaller fission weapons, was at this point brought into play to offset the lack of conventional forces. This appeared to make it possible to contain Russian expansion with conventional forces that, without it, would not stand a chance. At that stage the military were not thinking merely in terms of deterrence, but very definitely in terms of fighting a nuclear war. In 1954 Eisenhower told the US Joint Chiefs of Staff that they could plan to use nuclear armaments of all shapes and sizes in the future, wherever this would work to the advantage of the United States.[1] In a major lecture given at the Royal United Services Institute in London on 21 October 1954, Field Marshal Montgomery, then Deputy NATO Supreme Allied Commander Europe, said:

> I want to make it absolutely clear that we at SHAPE [Supreme Headquarters, Allied Powers, Europe] are basing all our operational planning on using atomic and thermonuclear weapons in our defence. With us it is no longer: 'They may possibly be used.' It is very definitely: 'They will be used, if we are attacked.' The reason for this action is that we cannot match the strength that could be brought against us unless we use nuclear weapons; and our political chiefs have never shown any great enthusiasm in giving us the numbers to be able to do without using such weapons.... If ever war should come again to this distracted world, which God forbid, weapons of power unprecedented in the annals of war are available for employment. There are some who say that if war is joined, nuclear weapons will not be used; I would disagree with that. My opinion is that the fear of atomic and thermonuclear weapons is a powerful deterrent to war; but once a world hot war has started *both* sides are likely to use them. We would certainly use them ourselves

[1] NSC-162/2, quoted by Mandelbaum, *The Nuclear Question*, p. 51.

if we are attacked, as I have said.[1]

Having said that in a war that came about by miscalculation, NATO would have to fight with what it had available at the time, he suggested that a deliberately planned world hot war would follow three phases:

First Phase: a world-wide struggle for mastery in the air and of the oceans. It will be vital during this phase to prevent enemy land forces overrunning and neutralizing Western bases and territories.

Second Phase: the destruction of the remaining enemy land forces.

Third Phase: the bargaining phase, when the enemy's homeland and all it contains is at the mercy of the Western air power. We will then carry the air attack to the point where the enemy accepts our terms.

The second and third phases may be concurrent.[2]

The thoughts of the staff at SHAPE about how NATO's armies would carry out the tasks of 'preventing the enemy land forces overrunning and neutralizing Western bases and territories' and subsequently of destroying the remaining land forces were based on the use of nuclear weapons, which it was assumed would be delivered by aircraft. In those days, before Germany had been rearmed and had joined NATO, SHAPE's plan was to defend the Rhine. The concept was that the river line should be held sufficiently strongly to force the enemy to launch a major operation to cross it, the defending troops preferably being from the country through which the river ran. Immediately behind that would be an empty zone, in which atomic weapons would be used to destroy the enemy forces as they emerged from the river crossing, while behind that again would be

[1] Text of lecture in author's possession.
[2] ibid.

NATO armoured divisions to deal with any forces that had escaped the nuclear bombardment. It was hoped that there would be time to evacuate all the civilians from the 'killing zone' before it was used as such, although it was realized that the refugee problem would be a severe one.

Although the possibility of the enemy also using nuclear weapons against not only our forces but also ports, airfields and other military installations on which they depended was taken into account, it was not considered very seriously, as it was thought that NATO was so superior in numbers of nuclear weapons and aircraft with which to deliver them that it would come off best. Attempts were made to devise organizations which would retain their operational effectiveness even under nuclear attack. The French Brigadier-General André Beaufre, then head of the Inter-allied Tactical Study Group, developed concepts for this, as did the American General James Gavin. Both plans involved a high degree of dispersion and were not very convincing as effective military solutions, and one important conclusion was most unwelcome to the politicians. This was that to be able to survive under nuclear attack and still be militarily effective, one needed larger, not smaller, armies.

These ideas, resting on an assumption of assured superiority in the field of nuclear arms, were given a sharp knock on 4 October 1957, when the Russians launched into space Sputnik I, an unmanned radio-transmitting satellite, followed a month later by Sputnik II, manned by a dog. They were clearly leading the world in the field of ballistic missiles, while the United States had continued to rely primarily on aircraft as the means of delivery of her nuclear weapons. The anxiety this aroused spurred the debate about nuclear strategy and the United States' defence policy in general, which had already been stirring in military, scientific and academic circles behind the scenes. The army had been unhappy at the priority given to the air force and to nuclear rather than conventional forces. Neither General

Ridgway, Chief of the Army Staff, nor his successor, General Maxwell D. Taylor, had much faith in massive retaliation as a realistic policy, and the latter urged the acceptance of a strategy of 'flexible response', which he expounded in his book *The Uncertain Trumpet*[1] after his retirement in 1959. He believed that the United States, and NATO also, should provide forces that were capable of meeting a challenge anywhere in the world on a scale and in a manner appropriate to the circumstances, all the way from guerrilla warfare to nuclear war. To prepare only for the latter would render them helpless to meet any other threat.

Liddell Hart was one of the first to draw attention to the futility of relying on nuclear war as 'a continuation of policy by other means'. The effects of strategic air attacks in the Second World War had led him to revise the views he had put forward between the wars as far as suggesting a direct attack against enemy cities was concerned. He had been an opponent of unconditional surrender and turned increasingly to consider methods of waging war that did not ruin the countries engaged in it. He was one of the first to adopt a sympathetic attitude towards the Germans once the war was over, partly influenced by admiration for their military professionalism and by the fact that their generals had put into practice his ideas about mobile warfare, which he considered that the British and French had neglected.

In an important lecture, which he gave in September 1957 under the title of 'Basic Problems of European Defence', he criticized NATO for thinking only in terms of nuclear war and for not preparing to meet other threats:

> At present the Western Powers' capacity for nuclear retaliation should suffice to deter Russia from launching a large-scale invasion of free Europe, or from attempting to paralyse the Allies' retaliatory power by a surprise blow. But, unfortunately, this power of retaliation is far less

[1] New York: Harper & Row, 1959.

> sure of proving a deterrent to smaller-scale aggression. It is thus much less of an insurance against the risk of an unintentional slide into an all-out war of mutual suicide.
>
> This risk will be increased if the Russians should become increasingly confident that they have secured a definite lead in developing long-range rockets—that might tempt them to take a bolder and more provocative line of foreign policy.
>
> Meanwhile the risk is certainly being increased by the way the military heads of NATO have tended to concentrate on planning and preparing for all-out nuclear war, without taking due account of more limited but more likely forms of aggression.[1]

Having criticized Field Marshal Montgomery's 1954 lecture, saying that to speak of winning wars and battles was an out-of-date concept in the atomic age, he went on to say:

> The military heads of the Western Alliance have been very slow in realizing the need of giving Governments and people some reason to hope that the defence, if put into operation, will not automatically entail suicide. Nothing could be more damping to the determination, and more conducive to hesitation, than the public statements that the heads of SHAPE have made about their plans. They have created a widespread, and still persisting, impression that they are planning to loose off nuclear weapons immediately in case of *any* attack—and not only against the attacking forces but against the countries behind.
>
> The announcement of such plans has naturally increased the uneasiness of the peoples of free Europe, in view of the vulnerability of their own cities and more densely populated countries to nuclear devastation—which they may also suffer from nuclear weapons used in their defence. It sounds all too like an insane reversal of

---

[1] Liddell Hart, *Deterrent or Defence* (London: Stevens, 1960), p. 55.

the proverb 'Those who live in glass houses should not throw stones.'[1]

He maintained that the principal risk was not the all-out premeditated attack, but 'local and limited types of aggression', and that if these were not quickly and effectively dealt with, the danger would be that they would develop, unintended by either side, into an all-out war. 'The prime need today,' he said, 'is to reinforce the H-bomb deterrent, which has turned into a two-edged threat, by developing a non-nuclear fireguard and fire-extinguisher—on the ground and ready for use without hesitation or delay.' In summing up, he added: 'To aim at winning a war, to take victory as your object, is no more than a state of lunacy. For a total war, with nuclear weapons, would be fatal to both sides.'[2]

He developed this theme in other lectures which were brought together in *Deterrent or Defence*. He was very nearly persuaded by General Gavin and others that there was less objection to nuclear weapons of very limited yield. Not only would they do little more damage to civilians, especially if airburst to reduce fall-out, than the air bombardments of the Second World War, but they would pose less danger of escalation to all-out nuclear war. Liddell Hart toyed with the idea, but on reflection came down against their use. In chapter 7 of *Deterrent or Defence,* entitled 'Are Small Atomic Weapons the Answer?', he pointed out that, on the assumption that they were used by both sides, they did not necessarily favour the defender. The need for dispersion would affect both sides. He doubted if the advantage they might bring in discouraging the attacker from concentrating too great a force in a restricted space outweighed this disadvantage and the fact that their use would be the first step in a process that could escalate. He concluded with these words:

---

[1] ibid., p. 57.
[2] ibid., p. 66.

> In theory, these small-yield weapons offer a better chance of confining nuclear action to the battle-zone, and thus limiting its scale and scope of destructiveness—to the benefit of humanity and the preservation of civilization. But once any kind of nuclear weapon is actually used, it could all too easily spread by rapid degrees, and lead to all-out nuclear war. The lessons of experience about the emotional impulses of men at war are much less comforting than the theory—the tactical theory which has led to the development of these weapons.[1]

Another distinguished thinker, the American Dr Henry Kissinger, had been giving thought to the same problem. He also recognized that the development of the Soviet Union's capability to retaliate against the American continent had undermined the threat of massive retaliation to meet lesser threats, and that the reliance of American and NATO defence policy on preparing only for all-out nuclear war had made both incapable of meeting other contingencies and unwilling to oppose any form of aggression, if the result was always to be a nuclear war. A student of Clausewitz, he saw force and the threat of it as an essential element in the 'political intercourse' between sovereign states: that there was no clear dividing line between policy and strategy. By preparing only for an all-out nuclear war, and the capability to fight one, the United States was denying herself the possibility of exercising her undoubted power in her own interests and those of her allies: she was unable to pursue an effective foreign policy.

He therefore advocated acceptance of the desirability of being able to fight limited wars, and stressed the urgency of developing the capability to do so, principally by the provision of air-mobile land forces and all that was needed to transport them to the scene of action and maintain them there. An invulnerable nuclear retaliatory force was the essential secure base from which to operate such a strategy.

[1] ibid., p. 81.

In his book *Nuclear Weapons and Foreign Policy*, he wrote:

> The dilemma has been defined as the choice between Armageddon and defeat without war. The enormity of modern weapons makes the thought of all-out war repugnant, but the refusal to run any risks would amount to handing the Soviet leaders a blank check. We can overcome the paralysis induced by such prospects only if our strategy can pose less absolute alternatives to our policy-makers. To be sure, we require at all times a capability for all-out war so great that by no calculation could an aggressor hope to destroy us by a surprise attack. But we must also realize that a capability for all-out thermonuclear war can only avert disaster. It cannot be employed for positive ends. We thus return to the dilemma which has plagued all our post-war military thinking. Does the nuclear age permit the establishment of a relationship between force and diplomacy? Is it possible to imagine applications of power less catastrophic than all-out thermonuclear war?[1]

In developing his arguments in favour of limited war, he emphasized the need to force on to one's opponent the decision as to whether or not to initiate all-out nuclear war. The latter would be unwilling to take the risk unless, when he did so, he could be certain of eliminating one's ability to retaliate.

> The key to a successful policy of limited war is to keep the challenge to the opponent, whether diplomatic or military, below the threshold which would unleash an all-out war. The greater the risk in relation to the challenge, the less total the response is likely to be. The more the challenge approximates the risks posed by all-out war, the more difficult it will be to limit the conflict. A policy of limited war therefore presupposes three conditions: the ability to generate pressures other than the threat of all-

[1] New York: Harper, 1957, p. 131.

> out war; the ability to create a climate in which survival is not thought to be at stake in each issue; and the ability to keep control of public opinion in case a disagreement arises over whether national survival is at stake. The first condition depends to a considerable extent on the flexibility of our military policy; the second on the subtlety of our diplomacy; the third will reflect the courage of our leadership.[1]

Having established the desirability of developing both a willingness to engage in limited wars and the military capability to do so, he then faced the question as to whether such wars should be limited to conventional forces or should involve a limited use of nuclear weapons. He rejected the former:

> A decision to refrain from using them would place Eurasia at the mercy of the Soviet bloc, at least in an interim period while we were readjusting the planning of our military establishment and redirecting the equipping of our forces. Then, too, there are some applications for nuclear weapons that it will be very difficult to discard, for example, the employment of atomic warheads for anti-aircraft missiles. Should this defensive employment of nuclear weapons be admitted, however, it will set in motion pressures for their offensive use. As attacking planes become more vulnerable, they must carry larger bomb loads, and the most efficient explosives are nuclear weapons. Thus conventional war will soon become the most 'unnatural' war and the most difficult to plan. A decision to rely on conventional forces in resisting local aggressions committed by a major power would represent a drastic break with present trends in the United States and among our allies.
>
> Moreover, in a war against a nuclear power the decision between conventional and nuclear weapons is not entirely

---

[1] ibid., p. 170.

> up to us. An aggressor will always be able to shift to nuclear weapons even in a war which starts out as a conventional war, perhaps by using initially weapons of very low yield.[1]

He pointed out that a force that was organized and deployed to fight conventional operations would be extremely vulnerable to the enemy's use of nuclear weapons against it, and recommended that NATO's forces in Europe should be designed primarily to fight a limited nuclear war. His concept for this followed the pattern that Beaufre and Gavin had suggested, that of a large number of small detachments, some static and others transported by 'low-flying aircraft', which, scattered in pepper-pot fashion all over the area occupied by the enemy's forces, would attack the latter with comparatively low-yield nuclear weapons. How they were to find their targets and co-ordinate their activities, what they would do after they had fired their weapons, and what the enemy's reaction was likely to be were by no means clear. There were few soldiers or airmen who thought it would be a practical or effective method of waging war.

An essential element of Kissinger's proposal was that 'by diplomacy' the opponent must be made to understand in advance that this curious nuclear game was not intended to be an all-out nuclear war, although the threat that it might turn into one, if he did not abide by the rules, had to be maintained. He realized that, if both sides played the game, it was not necessarily evident that the defender would win. He fell back on the dubious argument that the Americans were likely to win because 'our superior industrial potential, broader range of technology and the adaptability of our social institutions should give us the leadership.' And, 'Even should the Soviet Union overcome its difficulties in producing the required spectrum of weapons—and over a period of time it undoubtedly can do so—it will still be handicapped by the nature of its institutions and by its

---

[1] ibid., p. 176.

historical experience."[1]

Although NATO did not adopt the tactical concept that Kissinger had outlined, its Council formally decided on 17 December 1954 to base its strategy on the use of tactical atomic weapons. Six months after it had done so, in the month following Germany's entry into the alliance, a tactical exercise, tactlessly named Carte Blanche, was held by the Allied Tactical Air Forces in Central Europe, in which a total of 335 nuclear bombs were theoretically dropped in the area covering Holland, Belgium, West Germany and eastern France. This began an argument, which has continued ever since, as to whether Germany's contribution to the defence of Western Europe would not merely result in her total destruction if tactical nuclear weapons were used in her territory by both sides.

Kissinger's confidence in America's technical superiority was rudely shattered by the USSR's launching of the Sputniks. Even before that, he and others were aware of Soviet progress in the field of ballistic missiles, and fear of a 'missile gap' appearing in the 1960s caused him and others to revise their thinking, which had been based on the assumption that the means of intercontinental delivery by both sides would be long-range aircraft, against which it was possible to provide defence, including the use of nuclear warheads for anti-aircraft missiles. The same thinking had applied to Europe. Now Europe was faced with an immediate, and America with an imminent, threat of attack by weapons against which there was no defence, and to which aircraft bases, on which they relied for retaliation, were particularly vulnerable. Khrushchev's threat during the Suez crisis in 1956 to attack London and Paris with these weapons caused the penny to drop more than ten years after V-2s had landed on London.

In his book *The Necessity for Choice*,[2] Kissinger

---

[1] ibid., p. 194.
[2] London: Chatto & Windus, 1960.

emphasized even more strongly than before the need for an invulnerable retaliatory force and a capability to engage in limited wars, but he changed his mind radically about the desirability of fighting limited nuclear wars. He laid down three principles of deterrence. They were that the precondition of deterrence is an invulnerable retaliatory force; if the goal is stability, invulnerability should be sought through measures that convey, as far as possible, a defensive intent; and to maintain deterrence two errors must be avoided—one was to consider any given relationship as static, the other to subordinate present readiness to long-term balance in procurement. This led him on to point out that the more stable the intercontinental balance, the less effective was the value of a retaliatory force to deter limited aggression, as it would be 'foolhardy in the extreme' to threaten all-out retaliation to counter it. He rejected the arguments of those who proposed to overcome this handicap by developing a counterforce capable of destroying the enemy's retaliatory force in a first strike, on the grounds that it would lead to an uncontrollable and very expensive escalation in nuclear strike forces because, as they were regarded by the Soviet Union as a first-strike force, she was bound to respond in kind. There would then be no end to the race that would absorb defence resources to the detriment of those required to meet lesser and more likely threats. 'The only safe basis for planning strategy,' he wrote, 'is on the assumption of the mutual invulnerability of the retaliatory forces.'[1] Nevertheless he did not advocate total abandonment of any counterforce capability. His argument for it—somewhat far-fetched it may be thought—was this:

> If we have no counterforce capability whatever, an aggressor may attack our submarines and perhaps even individual missile bases in the United States while sparing our civilian population. For he may calculate that an American President would be loath to initiate a

[1] ibid., p. 38.

> campaign against cities which could not fail to have appalling consequences. To avoid these dilemmas, our retaliatory force must retain *some* counterforce capability—at least sufficient to deter a campaign of attrition against our retaliatory force.[1]

An important point he made was that the reaction of the two sides in a confrontation that threatened to escalate to war would be based on the relative importance of the issue to the two sides. The side that regarded it as the more important would be prepared to face greater risks and to climb to a higher rung on the ladder of escalation than its opponent, given that the mutual risks of war were more or less equal. In future years this was to apply to the Cuban crisis in 1962, when more was at stake for the United States, and to the invasion of Afghanistan in 1979, which was of greater importance to the Russians. Any incident involving the Germanies, including Berlin, would be of equal importance to both.

In discussing the controversial question of whether ambiguity about one's intentions added to or detracted from the credibility of one's deterrent posture, Kissinger came down on the side of making one's intentions clear. He did not deny that ambiguity could have its value, but insisted that it must be confined to the centre of the spectrum:

> It is essential to be clear about the range of uncertainty which is acceptable. The lower limit must *not* include the possibility of yielding or of a resistance so feeble that aggression is encouraged. The upper limit must not pose a threat which is either incredible or which would provoke a pre-emptive attack if believed. The lower limit of uncertainty should set the minimum price unacceptably high and, while keeping the maximum price open, avoid giving the impression of an automatism which is out of control once force is used.[2]

---

[1] ibid., p. 39.
[2] ibid., p. 55.

When he turned to the subject of limited war, he made his opposition to relying only on the threat of all-out nuclear war abundantly clear in a number of telling phrases, of which the most important were the following:

> The challenge before our military policy is to strike the best balance between deterrence and the strategy we are prepared to implement should deterrence fail. . . . We must enter it [limited war] prepared to negotiate and to settle for something less than our traditional notion of complete victory. . . . It only fudges the issue to look at the limited-war establishment primarily as a trigger for the retaliatory force. The free world will not really be safe until it can shift on to the aggressor the risk of initiating all-out war. . . . Deterrence is the art of posing the maximum *credible* risk. In the age of nuclear plenty and growing missile forces this is more likely to be provided by a strategy of limited war than by a retaliatory threat always in danger of becoming an empty pose.[1]

He postulated three requisites for a strategy of limited war: the forces must be able to prevent the potential aggressor from creating a *fait accompli*; they must be of a nature to convince the aggressor that their use, while involving an increased risk of all-out war, is not an inevitable prelude to it; and they must be coupled with diplomacy which succeeds in conveying that all-out war is not the sole response to aggression and that there exists a willingness to negotiate a settlement short of unconditional surrender. As for the actual forms of limited war, he considered and rejected three possibilities. The first was limited strategic nuclear war, or graduated retaliation: that is, using part of one's strategic force to attack a few selected targets in the enemy's territory. He rejected this as running too high a risk of becoming an all-out nuclear exhange, in which the initiator might suffer most. The second was indirect

---

[1] ibid., pp. 58, 62, 63, 64.

retaliation: that is, taking the offensive against the enemy in an area different from that in which the aggression has taken place, but in which the military factors are in one's favour. He rejected this because it also runs a high risk of escalation, especially for those countries in the area in which one has assumed the offensive, while contributing nothing directly to help those who have been attacked. The third was guerrilla or partisan warfare. This he rejected both because it would be unlikely to deter the aggressor or force him to withdraw, and also because it would impose a long-drawn-out internal division on the country concerned, which would be more likely to damage it than its invader. He came down in favour of putting a greater effort into local defence.

He then returned to the question of whether nuclear weapons should be used. He recognized that in a war between nuclear powers, whatever form it took, even if no nuclear weapons were used, both sides would have to take into account that they might be. The choice between conventional or nuclear weapons was not a one-sided affair. Even if the United States or NATO preferred to resist with conventional weapons, they had to be prepared for nuclear war as well, otherwise there would be a strong temptation for the aggressor to use nuclear weapons. He then explained why he had discarded his previous advocacy of preparing to fight a limited nuclear war, even one using nuclear weapons of such reduced yield that they were less destructive than some conventional weapons. His first reason was the inability of the US armed forces to agree on how a limited nuclear war would be fought—if they could not agree on a strategy and tactics for it, there was clearly little hope of establishing an agreed NATO strategy, and even less of being able to rely on accepted ground rules with the Soviet Union, which has always maintained that there could be no such thing and that any use of nuclear weapons would lead to their unlimited use. His second reason was the growth of the Soviet nuclear stockpile and the increased significance of ballistic missiles. His previous assumption that the Russians lagged so far behind that they could not maintain both large conventional forces and an all-embracing nuclear arsenal was being proved unfounded. As a result, he wrote:

> A nuclear strategy will now have to be conducted against an equally well-equipped opponent. Because of the destructiveness of nuclear weapons, the casualty rate among combat units is likely to be high. The side which has the more replacements available therefore stands to gain the upper hand. The notion that nuclear weapons can substitute for numerical inferiority has lost a great deal of its validity.[1]

His third reason was public pressure against reliance on nuclear weapons, which he attributed to arms control negotiations, rather than the other way round. He accepted that this influenced the framework in which any strategy had to be conducted and helped to determine the political cost.

He therefore came down firmly in favour of a significant improvement in the strength and capability of American and NATO conventional forces. He rejected the argument that this would undermine the credibility of the nuclear deterrent, and insisted that in order to deter the enemy from the use of nuclear weapons, these conventional forces must be backed by the capability to fight a limited nuclear war. But he deprecated the distribution of battlefield nuclear weapons to a low-level command as likely to lead to their use when it was unnecessary and undesirable, recommending that they be kept in special units under direct central control. He rejected very low-yield weapons on the grounds that the chief motive for using nuclear weapons was their destructive power; nuclear weapons that were no more destructive than conventional ones would not be worth the increased risk of escalation inherent in the initiation of their use. There would inevitably be difficulties

---

[1] ibid., p. 83.

in defining the limits of the war in such a way as to ensure that it remained limited. The least uncertain methods would be to make a clear distinction between conventional and nuclear weapons and to observe national frontiers as marking the limits of the operational area. But, at least as far as Europe was concerned, it was not necessary to be precise in defining, in the abstract, the line of demarcation between local defence and all-out war.

> The more effective the military establishment on the Continent, the larger must be the Soviet attack designed to overcome it. The more the required effort approaches the scale of all-out war, the clearer will be the challenge, and the more plausible the threat of all-out war becomes. The most favourable situation would exist if the military establishment in Europe could not be overcome locally. Then the risk of initiating all-out war would be shifted to the Soviet Union. At the very least, the forces in Europe should be sufficient so that the scale of effort required to overcome them raises the risk of all-out war to an intolerable level for the USSR.[1]

He maintained that, given the will, there was no reason why the financial, industrial and manpower resources of Western Europe should not provide the strength of conventional forces needed. As long as NATO's strategy relied on almost automatic nuclear retaliation, and as long as that was under the control of the USA—and to a lesser extent of Britain—other members of NATO were reluctant to accept the need for greater effort by them. They suspected that any increase in their conventional forces might be used as an excuse for reducing the strength of US forces stationed in Europe, and the prospect of a prolonged conventional war in Europe was little more attractive to them than that of a nuclear war. In the last resort Britain (and later France) could at best tip the scales in deterring

---

[1] ibid., p. 107.

the Soviet Union from starting a war at all, and at worst preserve their countries from nuclear attack, if not from any other form of attack.

Kissinger's answer to this was to call for radically greater political integration within NATO, at any rate among its European members. He proposed an agreement on the following lines:

(a) A political mechanism should be created empowered to make binding decisions for NATO as a whole in certain specified fields, particularly NATO strategy, arms control and those negotiations with the Soviet Union that affect the entire Western alliance, such as the issue of Berlin, German unification and European security.
(b) The level of the nuclear stockpile available to NATO should be fixed periodically by the political body.
(c) Once the stockpile is determined, the United States should agree not to withdraw weapons without the agreement of this political body.
(d) The political body should determine the circumstances under which nuclear weapons would be released to SHAPE (the military command).
(e) The United States should earmark a nuclear force for NATO and place it under NATO command.
(f) The British and French retaliatory forces should be placed under NATO command, except perhaps for token units.
(g) The Allies should build up their conventional forces to the levels agreed upon under joint plans and should not reduce their forces assigned to NATO except with the agreement of the political body.[1]

His sense of realism seemed to have deserted him. There was no possibility that Britain and France, four years after Suez, would accept anything like that, and little chance of

---

[1] ibid., p. 122.

any other European member of NATO doing so, even if the United States Congress could be persuaded to accept it. He opposed the existence or future development by other NATO members of their own nuclear retaliatory forces. He assumed that they would not be invulnerable to a first strike. He noted that Britain did not seem to have derived particular firmness and resolution from her reliance on nuclear weapons and went on to write:

> Whether the reaction is overconfidence or a sense of futility, the growth of individual retaliatory forces is almost certain to weaken the cohesion of the Western alliance. The very act of creating an independent retaliatory force springs from a lack of confidence in either American understanding of the common interest or American willingness to run risks on behalf of its allies. Moreover, unless a country's retaliatory force is directly threatened, a powerful incentive exists not to run major risks on behalf of allies. Each European country will face in relation to its partners the inhibitions against resorting to all-out war which they have ascribed to the United States and which induced them to develop an independent retaliatory force in the first place. They will reserve nuclear retaliation for direct and overwhelming attacks on their national existence. In relation to all other issues, their relative weakness and greater proximity to the USSR will probably produce hesitations exceeding our own. By the same token each ally that may be fearful of being involved in a nuclear war against his will may take drastic steps to dissociate himself from his partners in tense periods. The result of a multiplication of national retaliatory forces must be the weakening, if not the disintegration, of NATO. Such a course will diffuse the risks while detracting from over-all strength.[1]

While Kissinger, Liddell Hart and others had been concentrating their attention on the effects on the defence of

[1] ibid., p. 114.

Europe of an apparent strategic nuclear stalemate, intensive studies were being undertaken in the United States, notably by the RAND Corporation, of the implications for nuclear strategy of the ability of the Soviet Union to attack targets in America with nuclear weapons of megaton yield, delivered by ballistic missiles. It was generally assumed that the American and Russian strategic forces cancelled each other out, or, as Liddell Hart had expressed it: 'Nuclear parity leads to nuclear nullity.' However, a number of eminent members of the American scientific community, among whom Albert Wohlstetter and Herman Kahn were prominent, realized that matters were not as simple as that. For one thing, scientific discoveries did not stand still. Development of nuclear weapons had already progressed, both in the United States and in the USSR, far more rapidly than anyone, except perhaps Bernard Brodie, had envisaged. There could be no guarantee that mutual deterrence would automatically be maintained. The other concept was that nuclear war need not necessarily be the uncontrolled 'spasm' that most people assumed it would be. It might not be 'all-out', and need not be if statesmen and the military men responsible for it clearly understood the logic of nuclear strategy. If the possession of nuclear weapons was to be of any value as a threat to use in influencing an opponent's action, the latter must believe that they might be used.

As Brodie had seen in 1946, the first essential was to ensure that one's ability to strike at targets in the enemy's territory, which were of such value to him that he could not accept that risk, could itself survive a preliminary (pre-emptive or preventive) attack. It did not make sense to employ all one's force in a first strike against the enemy, unless it could be certain of destroying his ability to retaliate. This reasoning led to the demand for a first-strike force, aimed at the enemy's strike force, backed by a second-strike force which should, as far as possible, be invulnerable. But to indulge in exchanges of this nature would make no sense. Even a first strike, aimed at the enemy's nuclear strike force, would cause immense destruction and horrific secondary effects. However, superiority in the first strike, and an invulnerable second-strike force that was large enough to inflict unacceptable damage on the enemy, could be relied upon to ensure the continued validity of the deterrent to Soviet nuclear attack on America. There were two snags to such a policy. First, that maintaining superiority of a first-strike force could involve a continuous escalation in numbers, as the potential enemy's strike force increased in response, and second, that it would give the Soviet Union the impression that the United States was planning to carry out a first strike. This might encourage the Russians not only to increase their force but also perhaps to develop an anti-ballistic missile defence, and so it would go on.

While hoping that pursuit of such a policy would be successful, these erudite men developed their ideas to consider what should be done if it failed. When Herman Kahn published his book *On Thermonuclear War*,[1] discussing the various options of how to conduct one, it caused an outcry among those who regarded it as unthinkable even to consider such a war. He therefore called his next book *Thinking About the Unthinkable*, making the valid point that if you did not think about it, you were likely to do all the wrong things, which could be utterly fatal if you found yourself facing a thermonuclear war or the prospect of one. In chapter 4, entitled 'Thinking about Deterrence', he wrote:

> The word 'use' is deliberately chosen to emphasize the paradox that we preserve the peace today by the threat of war. Americans tend to forget that the threat of war can be credible only if war could occur. When we deter the Soviets by the threat that, if they provoke us in a limited war, subsequent reprisals may blow up into an all-out thermonuclear war, we are deliberately or inadvertently

[1] Princeton: Princeton University Press, 1960.

> *using* the threat, and therefore the possibility of nuclear war. When we tell our allies that our Strategic Air Command protects them from Soviet aggression, we are in a sense *using* nuclear war.[1]

He emphasized the importance of having a retaliatory force which did not have to be launched at unrealistically short notice. It must not be 'trigger-happy'. 'If the strategic forces on both sides,' he wrote, 'are well enough protected so that there is no necessity for either side to make any rushed decision, and if the centralized command and control systems are reliable, it is difficult to see how a war could start inadvertently.'[2]

He went on to consider a whole series of scenarios and options, starting from a state of tension, arising out of what he termed 'subcrisis disagreement', and ascending a ladder of escalation with sixteen rungs, the last of which he called 'The Aftermath'. The penultimate one was 'Some Kind of All-out War', and the following long quotation from his description of that gives the flavour of the sort of action these academics envisaged in the international 'game of chicken' that a confrontation between nuclear powers would involve.

> Because of some incident or crisis, or as part of a planned aggression, the Soviets might threaten a massive attack on Europe and refuse to back down even though we went through the temporizing measures of evacuating our cities, alerting our Strategic Air Command, and augmenting our air defense. The Soviets might believe we would be deterred from attacking them. They might have calculated that even if we launched an all-out attack against their strategic forces they could still destroy 50 to 100 partially emptied cities in a retaliatory blow. Suppose the Soviets were to launch a large conventional attack in

[1] London: Weidenfeld & Nicolson, 1962, p. 101.
[2] ibid., p. 120.

Europe and we were to fight back with augmented conventional forces. There would then be two reasonable possibilities: (1) we hold, or (2) we impede the Soviet advance but do not halt it. Assume the latter possibility and carry the scenario to the point at which a military debacle for the United States and its allies is imminent. At this point we would have a number of choices: we could use nuclear weapons in the combat zone and hope that the resulting bomb damage to civilians (from either the enemy's weapons or from ours) would not be too great and that it would not escalate into either all-out war or strategic bombing in Europe; we could attack the Soviet Union; or, finally, we could accept defeat. Suppose now that we are not deterred by the Soviet threat of destroying 50 to 100 of our empty cities. We might believe the studies that indicate we could recover in about ten years from such a débâcle. Perhaps we would argue that if the Soviets are going to behave this way now, they will behave much worse after they have added Europe's resources to their own, and that this is a good time as any to stop them—delay will only make them stronger and us weaker. Perhaps we would not stop to read studies and make calculations but simply act out of a sense of obligation and outrage. Whatever the reason, suppose we were to decide to attack the Soviet Union.

While we would be reluctantly forced to risk those 'empty' cities, we would in no sense be eager to lose them. In such circumstances we might most sensibly limit our actions in a very careful and controlled fashion. We might hit missile bases in Siberia, Soviet bomber bases away from cities, identified submarines at sea, and in general any target that does not involve the destruction of important military assets, taking particular care to avoid civilians. If the Soviets happened to have a bomber base in such cities as Leningrad or Moscow, we might deliberately refrain from attacking it, even though this self-restraint might result in our suffering more damage in the long run. Alternatively, if we did attack such a base, we would most likely use relatively low-yield kiloton bombs rather than multi-megaton bombs, and thus greatly limit the bomb damage to the neighboring city. We might simultaneously point out to the Soviets that, since we had (successfully) damaged their strategic forces in our strike, there were now no possible ways in which they could win the war. We would point out that our only aim is the removal of their threat against Europe. We would ask, 'Do you really prefer to start a city exchange rather than accept our peace terms? Is this the right time for you to start trading cities when we have such a large military superiority?' If we had achieved enough of an advantage we could use the Five City For One threat.[1]

There were two principal schools of thought that rejected this approach. One considered that all that was needed was a 'minimum deterrent', a small invulnerable retaliatory force that could obliterate a limited number of the Soviet Union's major cities, but have no counterforce capability. Its sole purpose would be to deter nuclear attack on the United States herself—it could not pretend to do anything else—and other threats would have to be taken care of by the non-nuclear forces of her allies. One of the disadvantages of this concept was that it would encourage proliferation. But the principal body of critics of the 'Unthinkable' approach were those who doubted if the careful control of every stage of escalation and of the actual use of nuclear weapons could, in fact, be exercised even on one's own side, let alone that of the enemy. Both then and later the Soviet authorities made it clear that, in their view, once a nuclear weapon had been used, there would be no holding back. Their publicly stated policy was that nuclear war would not be and could not be limited.

When John Kennedy became President of the United States in January 1961, he was well versed in these matters, and one of the main planks of his election campaign had

[1] ibid., pp. 198–200.

been that Eisenhower's Republican administration had neglected the nation's defences and left it vulnerable to the 'missile gap'. Robert McNamara, whom he chose as his Secretary of Defense, had the intellect to grasp all the aspects of the problem and the determination to hack his way through the jungle of conflicting views and competing interests. Kennedy's term started with a flurry of activity in the defence field, with great stress being laid on the need to create an invulnerable retaliatory force that could 'survive a first blow and respond with devastating power'. This was to be achieved by placing half the US Air Force's long-range strategic aircraft on air alert, until the programme for the production of Polaris submarines and Minuteman ballistic missiles in hardened silos reached a satisfactory stage. The numbers and the rate of production of both were to be increased. Faced with the bill for this, McNamara ordered an analysis of the numbers needed to inflict unacceptable damage on the Soviet Union. The criterion adopted was not modest: the destruction of 50 per cent of her industrial capacity and 25 per cent of her population. This could be achieved with a retaliatory force significantly smaller than that planned, and McNamara had considerable difficulty in getting rid of systems that he regarded as superfluous and ineffective, notably weapons delivered by aircraft.

He succeeded in cancelling plans for a new long-range bomber, the B-70, and for the airborne missile Skybolt, which both the US and British air forces were relying on to prolong the life of their existing long-range bomber aircraft. The argument that a large element of redundancy in delivery systems was necessary to counter the possible damage from a Soviet first strike was confounded by the discovery from satellite photography early in Kennedy's term that the missile gap was a figment of the imagination. Indeed, by the end of 1963, in the period in which Kissinger and others had feared that the Soviet Union would be able to apply nuclear blackmail to the West because of her superiority, she had only 100 intercontinental ballistic missiles, while the United States had over 550, and that took no account of all the other nuclear delivery systems which, based in Europe, could attack targets in the Soviet Union. McNamara also resisted strong pressure to develop an anti-ballistic missile defence system, supported by a major civil defence effort. He was never persuaded that even if vast sums of money were devoted to defence of the nuclear delivery systems themselves, they would have more than a marginal effect in reducing what was bound to be unacceptable damage. He succeeded in going no further than authorizing research into possible systems. He did, however, concede the development of a counterforce capability, in addition to the 'countervalue' capability aimed at industrial capacity and population. The motives for developing such a capability were mixed. One was that it appeared to be a more humane form of nuclear war than attacking cities. Others were that it added a rung to the escalatory ladder that fell short of all-out nuclear war; it would limit the damage that the Soviet Union could inflict on the USA; it made more credible the American capacity to respond to conventional or limited nuclear aggression in Europe or elsewhere; and it would discourage the development of independent nuclear systems by other nations, both by reinforcing the American umbrella and by demonstrating that, if a counterforce as well as a countervalue capability were essential ingredients of a viable deterrent system, they were beyond the resources of nations other than the USA and the USSR.

The announcement of his intention to develop a counterforce capability in a famous speech at Ann Arbor in June 1962 met with considerable criticism, partly because it appeared that, in spite of a clear announcement by Kennedy soon after his inauguration that 'Our arms will never be used to strike the first blow in any attack',[1] the United States was

[1] *The Public Papers of the Presidents of the United States, John F. Kennedy, 1961* (Washington DC: United States Government Printing Office, 1964), p. 231.

developing a capability for just such a strike: only if the enemy's system was attacked before it fired could such attacks be effective. It was bound to provoke a response from the Soviet Union, leading to the limitless arms race of which Kissinger and others had given warning; any attempt at damage limitation would detract from the threat of 'unacceptable damage', which could make nuclear war more likely, and it was unlikely to be observed by the Soviet Union, as Khrushchev immediately made clear. In any case, the 'collateral' damage of attacks on delivery systems would cause almost as much damage to the population and infrastructure (certainly if the USSR attacked the USA in this way) as a countervalue attack. As could have been foreseen, Britain and France reacted adversely. The measure was seen as designed to dissuade them from developing their own systems at a time when American policy appeared to be weakening the nuclear umbrella.

The first indication of that weakening had been Kennedy's emphatic renunciation of 'first use'. This removed the threat that if the Russians invaded Western Europe and NATO's conventional forces were unable to hold them, the United States would retaliate with the use of nuclear weapons. Strong protests from NATO forced Kennedy to qualify his declaration by stating that although he would not engage in a first strike against targets within the Soviet Union as part of a direct confrontation between the USA and the USSR, he 'would reserve the right to bring that arsenal into play if the Western forces were being defeated'.[1]

But McNamara did not leave it at that. He followed Kissinger's revised line and pressed for a more significant effort to be devoted to conventional forces for use both within NATO and outside it, laying considerable emphasis on the need for airportable forces. He wished to see the nuclear threshold raised, if possible to the level at which it

[1] Mandelbaum, *The Nuclear Question*, p. 75.

appeared to him that it alone was credible, that of a direct threat by the Soviet Union to the United States. He was also anxious to establish the tightest possible control of the use of nuclear weapons in order to eliminate the possibility that the United States could be dragged into a nuclear war, either by another nation or by one of her own commanders, in a cause that did not justify the risks involved. On both these grounds he was opposed to any concept of limited nuclear war, and therefore to the employment of tactical nuclear weapons. He resisted any further development of the latter and would ideally have liked to reduce them as NATO's conventional strength was built up. He put his proposals forward in the name of flexible response, only to find that, as discussions within NATO developed, the original concept was distorted into that of graduated deterrence or controlled nuclear response. NATO's strategy would be to meet conventional aggression initially with a conventional response, but, if that failed, to start climbing, rung by rung, up the ladder of escalation, beginning perhaps with a demonstration nuclear shot, designed to convince the enemy that NATO was prepared to use nuclear weapons if things got worse, on through short-range battlefield tactical nuclear weapons, then through intermediate-range, aiming at targets outside the Soviet Union, and finally to long-range strikes at targets within the USSR, selected initially from among those excluded from an all-out war target list (military installations or oil refineries in areas far from Moscow were often suggested as suitable sites). It had all the disadvantages that had been identified by Kissinger and others of being associated with limited nuclear war, and, as with so many previous concepts, it glossed over the effects of the enemy's likely response both on NATO's armed forces and military installations and also on the concentrated areas of population—the ports and cities of Western Europe. The concept justified every type of nuclear weapon from the artillery shell, through the short-range missile and the aircraft bomb, delivered by both tactical and strategic air forces, including naval aircraft, to the long-range ballistic missile.

Throughout his term of office as Secretary of Defense, McNamara found himself frustrated by the pressures of the symbiotic relationship between the designers, scientists and laboratory engineers of the nuclear warheads, the developers and manufacturers of the delivery systems, and their sponsors in the three rival US armed services. This was marked by a tendency towards continuous proliferation in numbers and types of warheads and delivery systems, and also for new designs to exploit improving technology, an important impetus in the nuclear arms race to which Lord Zuckerman forcibly drew attention in his November 1979 lecture to the American Philosophical Society, entitled 'Science Advisers, Scientific Advisers and Nuclear Weapons',[1] and in his book *Nuclear Illusion and Reality*.[2] In spite of the introduction of sophisticated methods of scientific analysis, cost-effectiveness studies and function-oriented financing, McNamara was only partially successful in enforcing the priorities to which logical analysis had led him, and in the end his efforts were overtaken by the Vietnam war. By that time he had not succeeded in limiting the American effort in the strategic deterrent field, nor in persuading America's NATO allies to devote significantly more effort to their conventional forces. The result was that mutual deterrence between the United States and the Soviet Union was likely to be bought at an ever-increasing price, and that, even then, the nuclear stalemate it would produce would lack credibility as a deterrent to Communist aggression elsewhere, notably in Europe.

---

[1] *Proceedings of the American Philosophical Society*, vol. 124, no. 4, and London: Menard Press, 1980.
[2] London: Collins, 1982.

3

Cuba, Nassau and Beyond

Before Vietnam diverted attention from the great strategic nuclear debate, the United States and the Soviet Union found themselves confronting each other in a situation to which all the theories that had been bandied about in previous years should have applied, the installation by the USSR of intermediate-range ballistic missiles in Cuba, which could have delivered nuclear warheads on to targets in the United States. Contrary to many of the theories put forward, neither side started to climb the ladder of escalation: both were extremely careful not to provoke the other to do so. The use of force was as limited as it could possibly be, and not a shot was fired. The fear of nuclear war, not the threat of the use of nuclear weapons, acted as a powerful deterrent in a situation in which, in military terms, the stakes were not that high, although the issue was clearly of greater importance to the USA than to the USSR. The fact that a few missiles in Cuba could attack targets in the USA made only a marginal difference to the latter's vulnerability and to the Soviet Union's capability to deliver either a counterforce or a countervalue attack. Put to the test, the existence of invulnerable retaliatory forces on both sides exercised a strong influence for restraint. The result of being brought to the brink, and of facing the fear that one step could lead ineluctably to the use of nuclear weapons or the awful decision as to whether or not to use them, was to bring Khrushchev and Kennedy together in an attempt to limit the nuclear arms race and reduce the likelihood of nuclear war.

The first step was to seek an agreement on a permanent ban on testing new nuclear weapons. It was hoped that this would not only prevent other nations from acquiring them—the USSR being particularly concerned to deny them to West Germany and China, with whom her relations were becoming strained—but would also end the nuclear arms race between the two great powers and initiate a process of reduction.

The attempt to reach a comprehensive test ban, including underground tests, foundered on the rock of verification—the number and type of inspections that the Soviet Union would accept within her own borders. Khrushchev offered two to four on-site inspections and three automatic recording stations in seismic areas, whereas the Americans insisted on a minimum of eight to ten inspections, which must include aseismic areas, and did not accept that the proposed sites for the automatic recording stations were satisfactory. But both sides were anxious to reach some form of agreement, the attitude of the USSR being affected by the deterioration in her relations with China, and recourse was made to a draft treaty, which the Americans had previously proposed for a 'three-environment' ban, covering the atmosphere, above the atmosphere and the sea. This became the Limited Test Ban Treaty, signed in Moscow by the foreign ministers of the United States, the Soviet Union and Britain on 25 July 1963 and ratified by the American Senate before Kennedy's death in November of that year. It had been achieved by the methods advocated by Stimson, a direct negotiation between those primarily involved, excluding any form of supervisory international body. And it was to be the forerunner of other agreements about nuclear weapons, limited as these proved to be, including the Non-Proliferation Treaty, signed in 1968 and effective in 1970, the impetus for which had come from China's explosion of her first device in 1964, following that by

France in 1960. Neither of these countries was a signatory to the treaty, under which the existing nuclear powers agreed not to transfer nuclear armaments to other countries, and non-nuclear nations agreed not to acquire them on the understanding that the nuclear powers would restrict the expansion of their existing nuclear arsenals.

In the Strategic Arms Limitation Talks that followed, the two major powers agreed in 1972 (SALT I) on a limitation in numbers for five years, an interim set of 'target figures', which allowed the United States 1,000 ICBMs (land-based Intercontinental Ballistic Missiles) and 710 SLBMs (Submarine-launched Ballistic Missiles) on 44 modern submarines and the Soviet Union 1,408 ICBMs and 950 SLBMs on 62 modern submarines. Conceding this superiority to the Russians took account of the fact that the agreement excluded long-range bombers, in which the Americans were superior, as well as all the 'forward-based systems' in Europe and her surrounding waters. The United States was also assumed to have a significant lead in multiple warheads. In November 1974, an agreement between President Ford and Brezhnev at Vladivostok established 'guidelines' for a permanent agreement limiting the total of all strategic delivery vehicles, including strategic bomber aircraft, to 2,400 for each party. Of the ballistic missiles, land- and submarine-based, in this total, 1,320 could carry Multiple Independently Targetable Re-entry Vehicles (MIRVs). Discussions to finalize this agreement (SALT II) were initiated in 1977 and completed in 1979. The agreement, which has never been submitted to, let alone ratified by, the American Senate, reduced the total to 2,250 and went into greater detail about the distribution of MIRVs between different systems and the type of aircraft covered by the agreement.

Over the years the American attitude to proliferation has varied, although it has generally been disapproving. That of the Soviet Union has never changed. She has been firmly opposed and, unlike the USA, she does not permit her allies to man delivery systems, the warheads for which she holds in her own custody, to be operated on a dual-key basis. Initially the United States administration, and even more its Congress, was strongly opposed to Britain's developing her own 'atomic bomb', and the wartime collaboration, the continuation of which appeared to have been assured by a memorandum exchanged in November 1945, was finally and firmly ended by the McMahon Act, passed by Congress in 1946. This forbade the transfer of any technical information on atomic matters to another country and brought an end to discussion between the USA, Britain and Canada, which had not got very far. The United States authorities had at first taken the line that for them to continue to co-operate with the British in the development of atomic weapons or energy would prejudice the success of the Baruch Plan, but their main concern appeared to be one of security. They feared that information might get into the hands of hostile powers, either by unauthorized leaks and espionage or by plants, established in Europe, even in Britain, being overrun by 'the enemy'. Their fears were accentuated by the exposure of the British physicist Dr Nunn May in February 1946.

The only card in Britain's hand was access to uranium supplies. The denial of American co-operation was a spur to, but not the origin of, Britain's independent action. Preliminary decisions had already been taken, the final confirmation being given in the gloomy atmosphere of January 1947, when, in an abnormally severe winter, the country was suffering from a fuel crisis. The only authoritative voice raised against it was that of Professor Blackett, who favoured a renunciation by Britain of atomic weapons, armed forces designed for purely defensive purposes only, and a policy of neutrality between the United States and the Soviet Union. Professor Margaret Gowing, in her official history of the United Kingdom Atomic Energy Authority, makes this comment:

The British decision to make an atomic bomb had 'emerged' from a body of general assumptions. It had not been a response to an immediate military threat but rather something fundamentalist and almost instinctive—a feeling that Britain must possess so climacteric a weapon in order to deter an atomically armed enemy, a feeling that Britain as a great power must acquire all major new weapons, a feeling that atomic weapons were a manifestation of the scientific and technological superiority on which Britain's strength, so deficient if measured in sheer numbers of men, must depend. A bomb would not be ready in any case for five years, so that the decision was of the variety that was impossible *not* to take rather than of the type that must be taken for urgent and immediate purposes.

The decision was also a symbol of independence. It had not been taken as a result of the breakdown in 1946 of Anglo-American atomic co-operation. The decision to produce fissile material in the United Kingdom had been taken before this breakdown and was regarded as non-negotiable in any circumstances. If the Anglo-American agreements drafted early in 1946 had been endorsed, they would in no way have altered the decision to produce plutonium, though it is possible that they would have made it unnecessary for Britain to plan her own gaseous diffusion plant. The agreements in themselves had no provisions which would have assured a supply of American atomic bombs to Britain, thus removing the need for Britain to fabricate them herself. It is conceivable that if the agreement had been signed and if henceforth Anglo-American relations had been bathed in sweetness and light, arrangements might have been made for the pooling of atomic weapons production. But in view of the actual American mood at this time, such a possibility is not worth even a cursory exploration. As it was, American atomic attitudes in this period hardened Britain's resolution not to be bullied out of the business and not to acquiesce in an American monopoly; it encouraged her determination to be a nuclear power for the sake of the influence this was expected to give her in Washington.[1]

This decision did not put an end to efforts to overcome the obstacles to co-operation, and Britain continued to play her only useful card—access to raw materials. At one stage Attlee's government was prepared to abandon Britain's plan to develop her own weapons in exchange for co-operation in development of atomic energy, provided that the United States would maintain in Canada a stock of atomic bombs, which would be available for use by the Royal Air Force in time of war. Any hope of this deal being agreed was dashed by the exposure of Dr Karl Fuchs in February 1950. When Winston Churchill's Conservative administration came to power in 1951, greater emphasis was given to nuclear matters. After a special conference between the British Chiefs of Staff and atomic scientists in 1952, a global strategy paper, giving the views of the Chiefs of Staff, was presented to the government. Professor Gowing summarizes its conclusions thus:

> What of the British part in the atomic deterrent? The deterrent at present rested entirely in American hands. The document concluded that, largely for economic reasons, it must remain there. But, said the Chiefs of Staff, it would be quite wrong for the United Kingdom to take no share in it. It was not possible to rely on the Americans to deal adequately with targets not of direct strategic interest to the United States. 'We feel that to have no share in what is recognized as the main deterrent in the cold war and the only Allied offensive in a world war would seriously weaken British influence on United States policy and planning in the cold war and in war

[1] *Independence and Deterrence: Britain and Atomic Energy 1945–52* (London: Macmillan, 1974), vol. 1, p. 184.

would mean that the United Kingdom would have no claim to any share in the policy or planning of the offensive.' There is no doubt that the recent discussions in Washington on the use of the atomic bomb had seemed to prove the great political disadvantage Britain would continue to suffer until her own contribution entitled her to claim a share in controlling what might be the decisive strategy in any future war and in determining any peace terms.[1]

The Americans exploded their first fusion or hydrogen bomb in November of that year. Expert opinion had predicted that Britain's resources would prevent her from following the same road, but on reconsideration the decision to follow once more in the Americans' footsteps was taken, for the same reasons as those inspiring the development of the fission bomb. The decision was influenced by the Chiefs of Staff's appreciation that there could be no effective defence against nuclear attack and their reliance on a return to the air staff's belief that offence was the best form of defence, a policy that air operations in the Second World War had not altogether proved correct. High priority was given to the Royal Air Force's V-bomber programme—the Valiant, the Victor and the Vulcan—as the delivery system, and there was little further questioning of the value of an independent strategic strike force until nearly ten years later, when it became clear that the bombers, some of which were only just coming into service, would have difficulty in penetrating Soviet air defences to reach targets as far east as Moscow, and Britain's first attempt to produce a ballistic missile, Blue Streak, had proved abortive. This led to the decision of Macmillan's Conservative administration to buy the American Skybolt missile, to be fired from aircraft that could remain outside the main Soviet air defences.

A great deal of discussion had taken place before that decision was made, not merely as to what system to obtain in

---

[1] ibid., p. 441.

order to preserve Britain's independent strategic force, but also as to whether such a force should be maintained at all. All three services had been subjected to severe cuts after the Suez affair. If the air force's share of the defence cake was to be maintained, the army would have preferred it to be concentrated on air transport, in order to implement the policy of meeting commitments outside Europe by the deployment of air-transported forces, now that the end of national service had been accompanied by a policy of doing without permanent garrisons overseas as far as was possible. The navy would have liked to see it devoted to maritime warfare, or preferably to be transferred to them to enable them to cope with the problem of keeping the surface fleet and the Fleet Air Arm up to strength and up to date. Mountbatten, when he had been head of the navy from 1955 to 1959, had not been keen that the navy should take over responsibility from the air force for manning the strategic deterrent force, fearing that it would mean the submarine element would absorb too great a proportion of the resources of men and money that represented the navy's share of the defence cake. But when McNamara abruptly cancelled Skybolt in November 1962, Mountbatten, then Chief of the Defence Staff, acquiesced in the decision to press the Americans to provide Britain with the Polaris missile to be fitted to British-built, nuclear-powered submarines, for which Britain would design and produce nuclear warheads. Kennedy reluctantly agreed to this at his meeting with Harold Macmillan at Nassau in the Bahamas on 18 December of that year. McNamara had to swallow the words of his Ann Arbor speech, describing 'limited nuclear capabilities, operating independently' as 'dangerous, expensive, prone to obsolescence and lacking in credibility as a deterrent.' He tried to get over this difficulty by insisting that the British Polaris force should be assigned to the support of NATO, preferably by incorporating it in the Multilateral Force, which the United States had been suggesting as a method of associating her European allies with her nuclear strategy without giving them the opportunity to act independently. The Nassau agreement stated that the British Polaris force would provide support to SACEUR (Supreme Allied Commander, Europe) and be targeted in accordance with his plans, and would also be 'available for inclusion in a NATO multilateral nuclear force', but Macmillan succeeded in adding the crucial qualification: 'except where Her Majesty's Government may decide that supreme national interests are at stake'.[1]

Successive American administrations had remained opposed to seeing other powers possess nuclear weapons, although contrary views had been expressed. At first Kissinger had been in favour, and had written:

> The possession by our European allies of nuclear weapons, on the other hand, will improve the overall position of the free world. It will make an attack by the Soviet Union on Western Europe an increasingly hazardous undertaking and it may improve the ability of the free world to hold other areas around the Soviet periphery. On balance, therefore, the diffusion of nuclear weapons technology will be to our advantage.[2]

However, when he later changed his mind on the subject, he enlarged on the topic:

> Independent retaliatory forces in Europe stand in danger of producing an illusory feeling of security which in some respects magnifies the danger. None of our European allies is capable of creating from its own resources a retaliatory force capable of defeating the USSR, *even* by striking first. For all practical purposes, then, the strategic striking power of the Soviet Union is invulnerable in relation to the retaliatory force of any European nation. Thus it is extremely unlikely that any

---

[1] Lawrence Freedman, *Britain and Nuclear Weapons* (London: Macmillan, 1980), p. 18.
[2] *Nuclear Weapons and Foreign Policy,* p. 198.

European country would retaliate by initiating nuclear war, even in the face of considerable provocation. For such an attack could not achieve victory, but would only guarantee the devastation of the country concerned. Europe is more densely populated than the USSR. The distance to targets in Western Europe from Soviet missile bases is relatively short. Compared with an attack on the United States, a retaliatory blow by the Soviet Union would therefore be more accurate and, because each missile would be able to carry a heavier payload, more destructive. Indeed, the Soviet Union might have a positive interest in ravaging the first European country that attempted independent retaliation against her. Reduced to rubble, that country could become a symbol, warning all others of the perils of opposing Soviet designs by means of nuclear retaliation.

Will retaliatory forces under national control at least be able to prevent nuclear attack against the country possessing them? Some people argue that the deterrent effect of an independent national retaliatory force does not depend on its ability to win. In order to deter, it need only be able to inflict damage out of proportion to any gain an aggressor might achieve. Yet, if the Soviet Union could be reasonably sure that the United States would not intervene in case of a challenge to individual European allies—which is, after all, the chief motive of our allies for building up independent striking forces—the national retaliatory strength in Europe would be likely to be overwhelmed by the Soviet blow. No European country seems capable of developing a retaliatory force strong enough to survive a determined Soviet attack. None of them has a sufficient area in which to disperse its forces or adequate resources to 'harden' them by placing them in concrete shelters—and hardening will be relatively ineffective or extremely costly against the accuracy possible in a Soviet missile attack on Europe. Indeed, until the retaliatory forces of our allies become mobile and

> preferably seaborne, they may constitute an invitation to Soviet pre-emptive attack. For any of our allies to attempt independent retaliation is almost certain suicide. The major utility of separate retaliatory forces in Europe would thus seem to be that they increase the aggressor's risk of American, not European, retaliation. They can deter only if the Soviet Union is convinced that conflict on a certain scale will unleash the United States' strategic forces. Far from making us dispensable, the effectiveness of separate retaliatory forces depends on the likelihood of United States intervention. Their function would not be substantially different from that of the tripwire. . . .[1]

It could be said that the use of ballistic missile submarines invalidated that argument, and his statement that they could only deter the Soviet Union if their use involved American strategic forces was to be used as a positive justification for their existence by both the British and the French, a concept that I have called the 'Trigger Argument'. Herman Kahn had opposed proliferation on the grounds that it would increase the difficulties of maintaining a stable balance and add to the dangers of conflict in international relations. He concluded a discussion of the subject with these words:

> In short, the diffusion of nuclear and other modern weapons could and probably will result in hazards additional to those we have today. The diffusion of nuclear weapons will probably increase both the number of crises and the seriousness and grim potentialities of any which do occur. Moreover, some governments will fail to take the proper precautions while others will try to exploit the common dangers for their own advantages. Under currently projected programmes this increase in hazards is unlikely to be compensated for by any change in the world of politics, and therefore one may expect an automatic increase in the probability that things will 'go

[1] *The Necessity for Choice*, pp. 112–14.

wrong'. Indeed an intolerable strain is likely to be placed on the present system.[1]

There is no doubt that one of the principal fears of the United States at the time of the Nassau agreement was that France, where de Gaulle had returned to power in 1958 and which had exploded her first device in 1960, would develop her independent nuclear force in some form of covert co-operation with Germany, and that this would not only arouse fears among fellow European members of NATO, but would be so intolerable to the USSR that she might be prepared to take the risk of military action to prevent it. Even if the fear of Franco–German co-operation was unjustified, de Gaulle could not be relied upon to pursue a policy in nuclear strategy or other nuclear fields of which the United States could approve. Given his deep anti-American prejudices, he might try to use France's nuclear power to pursue policies deliberately aimed against the interests of the United States. Hence the emphasis placed at Nassau, and in the negotiations that preceded it, on the Polaris deal being seen in the context of NATO and not as encouraging independence. But de Gaulle saw it in a different light, as one more attempt at establishing Anglo-Saxon hegemony and excluding France from power. Although the Nassau agreement has been represented as forcing de Gaulle to pursue an independent nuclear policy, he would almost certainly have done so in any case, and the spectre of secret Franco–German co-operation in the development of nuclear weapons was probably an illusion.

Whatever de Gaulle's motives, there was no doubt that the principal one was to emphasize France's standing as a world power, to be treated as an equal by the United States and Britain, and provided with the maximum degree of independence and freedom of action in international affairs. Deterrence of Soviet aggression in Europe was secondary, although it could be represented as significant in that

[1] *Thinking About the Unthinkable*, p. 222.

respect. One of those who presented it in that light was General Beaufre in his book *Deterrence and Strategy* (*Dissuasion et Stratégie*)[1] based on studies carried out by the French Institute of Strategic Studies, of which he was the head, in 1963–4.

Like Kissinger, Beaufre viewed with dismay the impotence that the stable strategic nuclear balance imposed on powerful nations. He saw it as having contributed to France's loss of Indo-China and Algeria. He believed that France, and the West as a whole, should pursue a dynamic total strategy, indistinguishable from policy, which would unremittingly employ every means to further their interests and ideology: these means should not exclude military ones, but for the most part they would be political, economic and cultural. It was essential to restore the discriminate use of force to the statesman's bag of tools. Nuclear weapons should have their place in this, as a threat and as a deterrent, not least to another nuclear power that might attempt to oppose the force one intended to use or to threaten. He recognized that the foundation of a credible deterrent was a secure second-strike force: both sides would then know that a first strike by either would provoke a riposte that was unacceptable, a situation which would deter both sides from using any force at all. Absolute instability was produced when each side was confident that, if it struck first, there would be no unacceptable retaliation. If only one side believed that, while the other feared unacceptable retaliation even if it fired first, the former side had achieved absolute superiority. If one side need fear only a limited retaliation if it were to strike first (that is, damage to itself that appeared acceptable in proportion to what was at stake), but the other feared retaliation that was unacceptable to it, the latter's nuclear retaliatory force might deter a direct attack on its own territory, but would not deter its adversary from anything

[1] Translated by R. H. Barry (London: Faber & Faber, 1965).

else. To ensure freedom of action, including deterrence of threats other than a direct nuclear attack on one's own territory, it was necessary to have nuclear superiority. One had to make it credible that one would be the first to use nuclear weapons.

When he addressed himself to what he called 'first-strike credibility', he concluded that, as things then stood: 'It would seem that in spite of counter-force or anti-missile tactics, the weight of both the American and the Soviet ripostes is enough to achieve a level of destruction far greater than anything which could justify the launching of a first strike.'[1] He then considered a policy of 'ignoring the irrationality' and proclaiming that a first strike would be an automatic response to certain actions by the other side—the massive retaliation concept—but, given the opponent's ability to retaliate to an unacceptable degree, he dismissed this as 'tantamount to suicide'. He then turned to what he called 'rationalizing the irrational decision', which was nuclear war limited to counterforce attacks, in the hope that the enemy would fear that his riposte to it would escalate to a second counter-city strike, the concept that McNamara had proposed at Ann Arbor and quietly discarded when he realized its implications, and which was to be resurrected in the days of Carter and Schlesinger as Presidential Directive 59 in 1974. Beaufre described it thus: 'The idea is that, faced with these increasing threats, one or other of the two participants would be the first to have had enough of this ghastly poker game and that the massive destruction of the paroxysmal nuclear exchange envisaged in 1955 would still have been avoided.'[2] He produced several reasons for discarding it, but came down in favour of what he called 'limited employment of nuclear weapons', probably as an adjunct to other operations.

Far from wishing to preserve a state of nuclear stability or balance, he wanted to create nuclear instability in order to

---

[1] ibid., p. 41. [2] ibid., p. 43.

maintain a state of mutual strategic deterrence embracing both the nuclear and the conventional balance of power. But clearly this state of instability must be one in which the West was superior in counterforce capability, through either a superior offensive counterforce capability or development of an effective defence against the opponent's offensive capability. 'Setting aside the subtleties, the variable truths and all the controversies,' he wrote, 'the keystone of nuclear deterrence is counterforce capability because only that capability, provided it is adequate, can make the launching of the first strike credible and because it is the threat of launching the first strike which constitutes deterrence.'[1] The fallacy in his argument was the one that McNamara had already perceived, as had Kissinger before that: that such a degree of counterforce capability was impossible to achieve, first, because to attempt it would provoke the Soviet Union to follow suit; second, because there would always be some part of the Soviet Union's nuclear delivery systems that would survive a first counterforce strike, notably hardened or mobile systems such as submarines, and because the other option—a sufficiently effective defence—was also impossible to achieve.

Beaufre then turned to multilateral deterrence, to what he called 'The Problem of the Third Party'. He quickly dismissed the idea that possession of nuclear weapons made it possible for a minor power to deter a major one, unless it were prepared to commit suicide. 'The only stake justifying suicide . . . would be complete loss of freedom—and even that is arguable: the disparity in the stakes can, therefore, lead to mutual deterrence on both sides, but if it is to do so, the stake must be total for the weaker party and minor for the stronger.'[2] He thus registered his disagreement with his compatriot, General Ailleret, who maintained that France's independent nuclear force was effective as a deterrent and as

---

[1] ibid., p. 49.
[2] ibid., p. 79.

a threat to '*tous les azimuts*'. Beaufre went on to show that the real value of an independent force lay in co-operation with a major nuclear ally. The minor power's force was protected against an opponent's first strike by the latter's fear of retaliation *by the major ally*, unless its force was also obliterated at the same time. The fear of action against the minor power's nuclear force or action by the latter starting a process of nuclear escalation, which could affect the delicate bipolar nuclear relationship of the major powers, would force the major ally to consider the interests of the minor power as its own. This was the true form in which possession of a nuclear strike force under independent control gave France its freedom of action—in Beaufre's view, as in Foch's, the true aim of strategy. It enabled France to pursue her own international policy, anti-American if necessary, confident in the knowledge that her nuclear force was inextricably bound up with that of the United States because the latter could not afford to let it act separately, and the Soviet Union could not afford to treat it as a separate force, action against which would not involve the risk of nuclear retaliation by the United States. This concept was the reason why McNamara was so opposed to such a force. It entrapped the United States into supporting France in some cause that it would have preferred not to, in order to prevent her from letting it lead to the risk of nuclear war. If she did not, France could even entrap her in a nuclear war, and yet it encouraged France to pursue an independent foreign policy that might be, and probably would be, anti-American. It was tantamount to blackmail—'a nasty word, loosely used to describe something which in fact happens all the time in international politics. . . . If certain means prove to be extremely powerful, there is no need to be ashamed of them nor to consider them dishonest. Other people would be quite prepared to use them if they had them."[1]

He developed the theme to show that independent

---

[1] ibid., p. 85.

nuclear forces within the alliance would strengthen it. They would bind it more firmly together, because the minor powers could force the United States to be more concerned with protecting interests that were of greater importance to them than they were to America; and, like France, they could be certain that the United States could not afford to dissociate her nuclear forces from theirs. At the same time it would add to the risks facing an opposing power. The latter could never be certain what action might not provoke one of the allies to trigger off nuclear action, and would have to be more careful to take into account their interests and reactions, not just those of its major opponent.

In the fashion of the French, Beaufre, although himself a very realistic man, wrote in terms of theory. He did not mention the problem of Germany, either what her reaction would be to all her allies having nuclear capability, when she was the main battlefield, nor what that of the Russians and their allies would be if she obtained it herself. Nor did he consider the possibility that if the other European members of NATO all started behaving like France, the United States might prefer to abandon the alliance. Once that happened, France's independent nuclear force, by his definition, would lose its value. But he did consider some practical applications of his theory:

> How in fact could we rely upon the judgement of an increasing number of statesmen, very few of whom would be qualified to shoulder so crushing a responsibility? The possibility of a madman being around is of course obvious, but more likely—and therefore more disturbing—is the possibility simply of lack of judgement: problems of peace and war have now become too subtle to be understood by every politician whom chance may bring to power; persistence of the traditional notions about war, now completely obsolete, must inevitably lead to catastrophes.[1]

[1] ibid., p. 97.

Like Britain, he preferred the process to stop with France. 'The proliferation of nuclear weapons must be stopped sooner or later,'[1] he wrote, and suggested that the threat of massive proliferation would probably force the major nuclear powers to act in concert to prevent it, and eventually that, 'Man's initiative will be canalized by this terrible disproportionate degree of power and in the long run it must inevitably reawaken his conscience and lead to the organization of a collective nuclear force as the secular arm of a true world authority.'[2]

Britain's justification of her independent force was seldom as clear, logical and coherent, but it was generally less cynical, although the air staff in particular had used Beaufre's 'trigger' argument. In 1955 Harold Macmillan, then Minister of Defence, arguing against relying solely on the American nuclear force as a deterrent, had said:

> Politically it surrenders our power to influence American policy and then, strategically and tactically, it equally deprives us of any influence over the selection of targets and the use of our vital striking forces. The one, therefore, weakens our prestige and our influence in the world, and the other might imperil our safety.[3]

A year later Britain's ability to influence American policy during the Suez affair did not appear to be affected by the existence of the V-bomber force equipped with nuclear weapons, although Beaufre's theory of interdependence could have been said to have been proved by the fact that Khrushchev's threat of Soviet ballistic missile attack on London and Paris was not taken seriously. However, many people, including Kissinger, thought that it had, and cited it as proof of the ineffectiveness of such independent forces as a deterrent. The target argument was soon quietly dropped, as it became clear that, with the increasing range of Soviet

---

[1] ibid.
[2] ibid., p. 99.
[3] *Hansard*, House of Commons, 2 March 1955, vol. 537, col. 2182.

delivery systems, there were no targets that threatened Britain specifically and, in any case, as the US nuclear arsenal increased, there was no lack of means to attack them all. The principal justification was distrust of the United States: in the event, she might not authorize the use of nuclear weapons to counter a conventional, or even perhaps a limited nuclear, attack on Europe for fear of retaliation against American cities. The Russians might believe this, and therefore would not be deterred from aggression in Europe by the American nuclear arsenal, even though part of it, as well as US conventional forces, was stationed in Europe. Finally, the United States might abandon Europe, removing both her nuclear umbrella and her conventional handle. The suicidal nature of a British (or French) nuclear posture of going it alone was brushed aside as unworthy of a nation that had stood alone against Hitler and endured the onslaught of his Luftwaffe. It was ironic that this, the principal British argument, was the exact opposite of Beaufre's contention that an independent force was only effective in combination with a major ally, although the 'trigger' element was common to both.

America's attempts to prevent further proliferation—to engage her European allies, but at the same time gain control of the use of their nuclear forces while keeping undivided control of her own in the form of the Multilateral Force—was seen by the Europeans for what it was. It was therefore as unpopular with the military, principally the navy, who considered it an ineffective and inefficient force that tied up the resources devoted to it, as it was with the politicians, who saw through the façade but were unwilling to reject it out of hand for fear of offending their ally, on whom they were so dependent. Some of them were still receiving US military aid. It died a quiet death in 1965, decently laid to rest on the excuse that its demise might encourage progress towards a Non-Proliferation Treaty. In its stead, European members of NATO were provided with a forum in which they could discuss nuclear policy by the establishment of NATO's Nuclear Planning Group, a six-monthly meeting of the Defence Ministers of the major NATO nations, the minor ones having to be content with a limited, rotating number of seats at the table.

Beaufre was emphatic that nobody wanted a nuclear war and that nobody would benefit from one that was anything worse than what he defined as 'sublimited nuclear war'.

> If there were no form of nuclear warfare thought to be practicable, the credibility of the nuclear deterrent would fall to zero. To preserve this credibility there must be at least one type of minor nuclear warfare capable of acting as the first step in the escalation process, or at least of causing people to fear that escalation might take place.
>
> This opens up the whole problem of first-strike credibility discussed at length in connection with deterrence.
>
> We have before us a spectrum as wide as it is varied, ranging from the bottom to the top level of violence; within it are two major subdivisions, 'non-nuclear practicable wars' and 'highly improbable nuclear wars'; this means that we must devise a type of warfare which can form the connecting link between the two categories. It must be both practicable—*in extremis*—and nuclear.
>
> This intermediate form of warfare would seem to be 'sublimited nuclear war'; in other words, a war involving the possible but very restricted use of nuclear weapons. How can any nuclear war be 'sublimited'? There are two schools of thought, a fact which shows how conjectural the whole concept is. Some people, Herman Kahn for instance, conceive it merely as a series of strategic warning shots purely psychological in purpose (bombs into the tundra or on Kamchatka, for instance). Others such as Kissinger, on the other hand, see these warning shots being directed on to tactical targets (to destroy an invading force or intervene in a defensive battle for instance). In any event the idea would be to use only a very small number of weapons, as opposed to NATO's

> tactical concept of recent years envisaging all-out employment of short-range weapons.
>
> Is this concept realistic? No one can say. It is certain, however, that it is the only method of preparing for a demonstration of our determination to embark on escalation with the object of avoiding this type of conflict. It must therefore be considered to be feasible and we must visibly be prepared to use it if we wish first to maintain the deterrent value of the nuclear system, and secondly to retain the ability to reinforce our conventional capacity on a considerable scale. Personally I incline towards the Kissinger theory.
>
> Indisputably, however, this connecting link is a 'must', not of course because we wish to use it but in order to deter, in other words in order to extend the stabilizing effect of the nuclear threat on the conventional level.[1]

In 1965, when Beaufre's book was published in Britain, the United States became fully involved in the Vietnam war, President Johnson authorizing an increase in US forces there to 125,000 and removing restrictions on their use. For the next ten years Vietnam absorbed the attention of the United States and of those elements in America and in Europe that might have continued to protest against strategies based on nuclear weapons. They were too preoccupied with protesting about the Vietnam war. When both turned their attention back to the subject, it was discovered that, in spite of a considerable increase in America's nuclear arsenal, and a build-up also of the British and French arsenals, it appeared that greater proportional improvements had been made in the Soviet armoury. A significant programme of ballistic missile submarines had given them a secure second-strike retaliatory force, which had also been improved by hardened silos for land-based missiles, now increasingly solid-fuelled. In the tactical field,

---

[1] *Deterrence and Strategy*, pp. 112–14.

defensive fighter aircraft in Europe had been replaced by fighter-bombers capable of delivering nuclear weapons—the longer-range Backfire bomber, not intercontinental without in-flight refuelling, had been added to forces that could be labelled as strategic—and battlefield weapons, principally missiles, had increased in numbers and range.

When Nixon succeeded Johnson as President of the United States in 1969 and brought Kissinger into his administration as National Security Adviser, both sides were intent on improving their nuclear arsenals, although in the case of the United States it was more in the form of plans for future improvement, whereas the Soviet Union was in a production phase, significantly increasing numbers of long-range ballistic missiles capable of putting heavy 'delivery vehicles' into and above the atmosphere. At the same time the Vietnam war had fomented a vocal anti-military lobby in Congress and elsewhere, providing not only strong opposition to military expenditure but also pressure for arms control negotiations to limit or reduce the escalating nuclear arms race.

The developments that the Johnson administration had initiated were a new submarine ballistic missile to replace Polaris, the Trident, a new bomber to replace the aged B-52, the B-1, a mobile Minuteman, the M-X, the cruise missile, which could be launched from land, air or sea, a resurrection of the ABM (Anti-Ballistic Missile) system that McNamara had dropped and, most significant of all, an extensive programme of MIRVs. The latter had been developed to defeat ABM systems, but, with the combination of a significant reduction in the size and weight of fusion warheads, the increased accuracy with which they could be delivered, and improvements in satellite photography that could exploit that accuracy, the possibility was opened up of making a reality of a counterforce strategy, which could at least deal with the Soviet Union's land-based missiles. As the number of launchers was likely to be limited both by the reluctance of Congress to approve increases and by restrictions that might arise from arms control negotiations, MIRVs could increase the United States' offensive capability without a significant and costly increase in launchers. The snag lay, as it had lain in other projects and was to continue to lie in the whole nuclear field, in the fact that the Soviet Union would sooner or later catch up and the advantage would be nullified.

Kissinger was anxious to go ahead with all the projects, particularly with an ABM system. Although frustrated by the lack of enthusiasm of Congress and the American public for significant improvements in strategic systems, he saw that a continuous spiral of escalation in strategic delivery systems would not provide additional security to the United States or the West as a whole, and that it was in the interest of the Soviet Union also to bring it to a halt. An arms control agreement should not just be accepted as a disagreeable necessity, forced on him by a war-weary Congress and people, but should be welcomed and worked towards for its own sake, provided that an agreement could be negotiated that would ensure the security of the United States herself and her interests overseas, including Europe.

As the negotiations leading to SALT I proceeded, and as they developed after 1972 towards SALT II, the ambivalent attitude of NATO's European members was once again demonstrated. On the one hand, they expressed their fears that the agreements would undermine America's superiority in strategic nuclear capability, producing a stalemate that prejudiced the credibility of the US nuclear umbrella over Europe. It was true that the agreements recognized a balance between the two opposing systems: without that no agreement was possible. But it was no more than a recognition of reality, in that striving for superiority was never going to succeed unless unlimited resources were to be devoted to a nuclear arms race in which the technical superiority of the United States was always likely to be balanced by the willingness of the Soviet Union to devote a greater proportion of her resources to it. On the other hand, when the arms race, or any other issue, led to instability, tension and bad relations between the two giants, the Europeans complained that America's bellicosity was needlessly increasing the danger of conflict. When relations between them were relaxed and the two sought agreements with each other, the Europeans complained that the giants were settling the world's affairs without considering their interests. Little wonder that Americans were frustrated in their dealings with their allies. However, the SALT agreements were generally welcomed in Europe, and disappointment was expressed when SALT II was not ratified.

Before the ink was dry on any of the agreements, there were plenty of voices raised by hawks complaining that they passed the advantage of superiority over to the Soviet Union, on the grounds that the latter's greater number of land-based missiles, with greater 'throw-weight' than the Americans', by exploiting the use of high-yield MIRVs, could destroy the Minuteman force in its silos. The Soviet Union could then threaten a first strike against that force, to which the only possible retaliation would be the use of submarine ballistic missiles against Russian cities. As this would invite retaliation against American cities, the President would not dare to threaten it and would be forced to succumb. The US Air Force's long-range bomber force of ancient B-52s did not appear to affect the issue, and it is no wonder that Carter refused to authorize its replacement by the B-1. The answer to the criticisms was twofold. First, to try to return to a 'no cities' policy, which, as always, had the disadvantages of all concepts of limited nuclear war. This was combined with the concept of 'limited use', the introduction of successive steps on the ladder of escalation, and was promulgated by the then Secretary of Defense, James Schlesinger, as Presidential Directive 59 in 1974. One of the motives behind it was to find targets for the increasing number of warheads. However, adding more cities to the extensive 'assured destruction list' made little sense, and was recognized as making inhumanity even more inhumane. The other answer to the critics, most of whom were Republicans, and among whom Ronald Reagan was prominent, was to do more to reduce the vulnerability of the land-based ballistic missile force, and a number of extremely expensive schemes to provide mobility were suggested. When Reagan came to power in 1981, he found the political and financial cost too high and compromised with a decision to improve the hardening of the existing Minuteman silos. Once more the search for superiority had proved illusory.

The strategic level was not the only one that caused problems. Two other proposed improvements of the nuclear arsenal aroused opposition in Europe and helped to fuel the reappearance of a determined anti-nuclear movement. One was the neutron, or enhanced radiation, weapon. This was an artillery shell developed to reduce blast and heat effects and to enhance radiation, which would reduce fall-out or, if airburst at the correct height, eliminate it and kill people and animals within its zone of effect with reduced damage to buildings. One of the motives behind its development was to make the use of tactical nuclear weapons on her own territory more acceptable to West Germany and therefore to make the threat of their use as a deterrent to conventional aggression more credible. As usual, the concept neglected the likely response of the other side, which could not be guaranteed to be equally 'clean' and limited. The weapon was presented ineptly as 'killing people and preserving property'. It was unjustifiably objected to as if it were worse than weapons that did both; but it was undesirable in that it tended to blur the distinction between conventional and nuclear war, making it more likely that the military would press for its use and the US President authorize it. When his European allies objected to its deployment on their territory, President Carter abandoned the project. However, Reagan has resurrected it.

The other project, which caused more trouble, was what

was called 'modernization of theatre nuclear weapons'. The Soviet Union's development and deployment of considerable numbers of the long-range, solid-fuelled, mobile, MIRVed SS-20 ballistic missiles to replace her old static, liquid-fuelled SS-4s and SS-5s, which could not reach the extreme west of Europe from sites in Russia as the SS-20 could, aroused two fears. One was that it made vulnerable the West's land-based systems in Europe, mostly aircraft bases; the other was that while the SS-20 could strike cities all over Western Europe, the only systems assigned to the support of SACEUR, which could retaliate on to targets in the USSR, were the American and British Polaris submarines used in that role. The American response to these fears was to propose the deployment of 464 Tomahawk cruise missiles to Western European countries, and, in addition, 108 Pershing II ballistic missiles to West Germany.

These proposals, and the British Conservative administration's decision in 1980 to replace British Polaris ballistic missile submarines with new submarines equipped with the US Trident missile, for which Britain would have to design her own multiple warheads, surfaced at a time when relations between the United States and the Soviet Union had deteriorated as a result of events in Iran and Afghanistan, and Reagan, who had made very hawkish statements about his attitude to the Russians during the Presidential election campaign in 1980, came to power in America. Protests against NATO's nuclear policy became widespread and influenced NATO to demand that the condition of acceptance of the cruise missiles and Pershing IIs was that the United States should attempt to reach agreement beforehand with the Soviet Union to reduce the Russian threat, if possible by removal of the SS-20s, making the deployment of the cruise missiles and Pershings unnecessary. Nobody had actually attempted to claim that the latter could counter the SS-20 in military terms, even in a first strike.

4

A Policy for Continuation

The result of the process described in the previous chapters is that there are now approximately 40,000—some put it as high as 50,000—nuclear warheads, more or less equally divided between the West and the Soviet Union, a slight majority, probably, in the hands of the former. Most of these warheads are of far greater destructive power and more dangerous in their immediate and long-term effects, especially the Russian ones, than the two dropped on Japan in 1945. When one considers how horrible was the destruction and suffering caused by those two, one is driven to the conclusion that the world has gone mad. Clausewitz would certainly have thought so. They could not possibly be used, not even a small proportion of them, in any war that could be called a 'continuation of policy', unless it were a policy of genocide and suicide. No wonder old and young alike protest against so-called defence policies that could result in their use. The actual use of any significant number of them is inconceivable—only people with no imagination can envisage it. In this situation, is war during the rest of the twentieth century, and in the twenty-first, likely to be effective and acceptable as 'a continuation of state policy by other means'? Before we can answer that question, we must consider what that policy is, what it should be, and where and in what circumstances the clashes of policy may occur that could lead to West or East considering that their policy should be 'continued by other means'.

Put in its broadest terms, the policy of the West is to preserve as much freedom as possible in as large a portion of the world as is feasible, certainly in Britain, in Europe and in those countries whose resources are relied on to maintain the standard of living of the large number of people crowded into these lands. Freedom to trade and exchange goods; freedom to travel, to work and to live; freedom to hold and express ideas and to exchange them with others—all with the minimum of interference by governments of our own or any other nation. Some would say that to preserve and maintain those freedoms is not enough; they consider that the West should pursue a dynamic or total strategy to enlarge the areas in which they can be enjoyed. They would like to orchestrate all the activities of every like-minded nation—cultural, economic and political, supported by military—to this end. Alexander Solzhenitsyn was one of these, when he said that the West was suffering from 'loss of courage' and 'loss of reason'; that its policy was one of 'calculated cautious hypocrisy'; that we were 'no more than a collection of cardboard sets, bargaining with each other to see how little we can spend on defence and how much we can spend on our comfort'; and that the greatest danger was that we had 'lost the will to defend ourselves'.[1] The aim of such a policy is without doubt desirable, but it has two disadvantages. First, it requires a degree of centralized control of these activities, both national and international, that runs directly counter to the freedoms that it seeks to establish; and, second, it is bound to lead to a direct clash with those who think differently, notably the Communist powers, and particularly the Soviet Union. If we wish to avoid pushing the furtherance of our policy to the extent of 'continuing it by other means', we may have to be content with preserving what freedoms we have and preventing them from being eroded. And that may be difficult enough.

What are the threats to these freedoms with which such a

---

[1] In an interview with Michael Charlton on BBC Radio, December 1976.

policy is likely to come into conflict? Basically, there are two. One is narrow nationalism, which tries to deny freedom of access to its resources, physical and cultural, to those outside its borders, and also, perhaps, to deny to its own people access to the resources and ideas of other peoples and nations. The other main threat is that of Marxism-based societies, of which the Soviet Union is at present the most powerful and threatening, which seek to impose a centralized, enclosed economy and organization of society. They put little or no emphasis on the freedom of minorities and individuals to choose their own way of life; all must be submissive servants of the state, which is itself the slave of the Party.

The first decision that has to be made in determining a policy intended to preserve and extend peace is whether to pursue an aggressive, dynamic strategy in an attempt to roll back the barbed wire that nationalism, Marxism or a combination of both erects to keep out freedom, or if that is likely to endanger peace, as it is, whether to accept that there is little we can do to change those frontiers, where they exist, and to seek instead as stable and peaceful a relationship as we can with nations of whose political, cultural and economic systems we deeply disapprove. For the sake of peace, perhaps it would be advisable to accept that a large proportion of our fellow human beings are denied justice, and that the best way we can help them is by encouraging a stable and peaceful world in which, following the ideas and example we provide, they may be able to change their society from within.

The choice between these rival policies depends on whether we assume that the Soviet Union is more or less satisfied as far as the extent of the territory over which she exercises direct control is concerned, or is, as some believe, 'your adversary, the devil, as a roaring lion, walking about seeking whom he may devour'. As far as Europe is concerned, the 1975 Helsinki Conference on Co-operation and Security in Europe seemed to show that the Soviet

Union believed that security in Europe depended on co-operation between East and West in preserving existing frontiers and not interfering with the internal affairs of the countries on the opposite side of the Iron Curtain—not, as many in the West saw it, as an opportunity to establish east of the Curtain the freedoms that citizens west of it enjoyed. Events in Poland have highlighted the difference of interpretation, and also the difference between the dynamic and the quietist approach to how the West should react to events within the Soviet bloc. In general, the Europeans, and especially the Germans, who have the experience of daily relations with East Germany, have tended to be restrained in their condemnation of the Polish Communist government and of the USSR, believing that abuse and pressure would not only lead to harsher treatment of the dissidents, but also be to the prejudice of stability and peace in Europe generally. The Americans, on the other hand, have been strident in their criticism and anxious to apply every kind of pressure except military, although reluctant to use one that is ready to hand—grain supplies. The fact that the centre of power in the United States has now shifted from the east to the west coast, 3,000 miles further away from Europe, no doubt accentuates this tendency, as does the existence of a large and influential element of Polish origin in her electorate. It is of great importance that NATO should resolve this internal tension between the two basic policies, for Europe, ideologically and politically, is where the clash of policy is keenest, the military forces strongest and in closest proximity and the results of 'continuing policy by other means' fraught with the gravest consequences.

There are those who suggest that the solution to this danger is to separate the two giants, who have no direct territorial claims on each other, unless the USSR were to demand the return of Alaska, which she sold to the United States in 1867. E. P. Thompson, leader of the European Nuclear Disarmament movement, is one of these. He advocates not only the removal of all nuclear weapons 'from the Atlantic to the Urals', but also the removal of all American armed forces from Europe and the withdrawal of Russian forces behind their frontiers. A similar suggestion is being bandied about within the Liberal Party, although its sponsors are not so unrealistic as to believe that there is any way of verifying withdrawal of Soviet nuclear weapons, within the Soviet Union, to the east of the Urals. Supporters of this disengagement maintain that there would then be no potential source of conflict between the states of Europe that could lead to war, a view that can only be regarded as naive in the extreme. Recent events in Poland alone, and their implications for her neighbours, are surely proof of that. But the overriding question mark would be over the future of Berlin and East Germany. Even if the Soviet Union were to agree, which is highly unlikely, and assuming that the withdrawal of both sides had proceeded peacefully and without incident, Europe west of the USSR's borders would then be overshadowed by her overwhelming military preponderance, no longer balanced by that of the United States beyond the Atlantic. If events in Eastern Europe then took a direction unpalatable to the Soviet Union, the fear of war with the United States would not restrain her from intervention. The threat of such intervention might alone suffice for her to gain her ends, and not only among her former satellites.

There are some military men, principally in the navy, who support this concept, believing that an American 'rapid deployment force', transporting troops by air and sea, could provide the necessary balance. Their view bears as much relation to military reality as the proposal by Admiral Jacky Fisher before 1914 that an amphibious landing on Germany's Baltic coast would be a more effective contribution to the defence of France and the Low Countries than an expeditionary force beyond the Channel. The Americans could not suddenly withdraw their forces from Europe. From the time that their withdrawal was first intimated, the political effect on the European members of NATO, not least the Federal Republic of Germany, would be overwhelming. It is inevitable that it would take the form of an *Ostpolitik*, which would result in an accommodation with the USSR's economic and political system. That is the only way in which it could be combined with peace. A policy must be pursued that preserves our freedom without too high a risk that the conflict of ideas may spread beyond words to deeds of violence.

Some suggest that the internal tensions of the Atlantic Alliance can be lessened by developing it into more of a twin-pillar alliance, the European pillar being provided either by developing the European Economic Community into one that embraces defence, or by strengthening the bonds that link the European members of NATO, so that they would act together to balance the influence of the United States in conventional forces, in defence procurement and, perhaps, in nuclear weapons, too. The drawback to this, even if France could be integrated into such a pillar, is that it would tend to encourage those elements in America who are already inclined to consider the possibility of withdrawal of their forces. There are also other European members of NATO, whose links with the United States are closer than they are with their fellow European allies, who would be reluctant to be incorporated into such a pillar. The presence of American conventional army and air forces in West Germany is the most important factor that links the power of the United States in all its forms to the security of Western Europe, at least as important, if not more so, than the presence of her nuclear delivery systems on the Continent. To satisfy the Americans that they should continue to station their forces in Europe, it is essential to persuade her politicians and people that the Europeans are playing their full part, that their forces are not a 'forlorn hope' and that they stand a good chance of succeeding in their task, making it worthwhile planning to reinforce them in an emergency. And the inadequacy of conventional forces in Europe should not force the American President to face the awful decision as to whether or not to initiate the use of nuclear weapons within a few days, or even hours, of the outbreak of war. Any policy designed to keep the peace in Europe must meet this need.

There are others who suggest that we in Europe are too mesmerized by the problems of the defence and security of Europe itself, and particularly that of the Central Region between the Alps and the Baltic. They suggest that the Soviet Union deliberately encourages the West to focus its attention on Europe, while it plans to outflank us by bringing about a situation in which the West is denied access to the oil supplies of the Middle East and the mineral resources of southern Africa, which are vital to the Western capitalist economy. It is true that our economy would be in grave difficulties if that access were denied. If all other measures to preserve access failed, I believe that we should be justified, in the last resort, in using military force to restore that access, whether it was denied to us on grounds of nationalism or of Marxist ideology, but we, in Britain, could not act alone. The West as a whole would have to be united in its resolve and to have been associated with the negotiations that had led to the impasse. The military forces employed would inevitably have to come principally from the United States, but we and other European countries should be prepared to play our part. Unless the action was on a very small scale, the forces we could provide would be little more than token, as they were in Korea. If such action were to risk direct conflict with the Soviet Union, a very careful balancing of the risks with what was at stake would be required, never an easy judgement to make at a time in which tension is high and emotions are strong, under the influence of anger and fear. The fear of nuclear war would be the greatest.

I would not wish to imply that I favour gunboat diplomacy as normally a good way of handling international affairs, certainly not in its literal sense. President Nixon was disappointed when the despatch of the 90,000-ton, nuclear-powered aircraft-carrier USS *Enterprise* to the Bay of Bengal in December 1971 made no impression on India's invasion of East Pakistan. The implications of the use of force at a great distance from one's own country, even if the opponent is small and weak, require careful consideration. Such use of force can only too easily be counterproductive, both nationally and internationally, but a helpless wringing of the hands is no policy at all.

Important as these areas outside Europe are, and the freedom to use the oceans and narrow waters that link them, I have no doubt that the overriding priority is to preserve the peace in Europe, and that the most likely cause of war there would be the instability created by any attempt to juggle the kaleidoscope through changing the rigid pattern of frontiers established at the end of the Second World War. To attempt to change them, or to entice one of the countries east of the Iron Curtain to take a step across it, would be a certain recipe for a Third World War. Even if nuclear weapons did not exist and had never been invented, with modern conventional weapons war could deal a death blow to European civilization. With the vast nuclear arsenal that exists on both sides today, it could almost destroy life in the Northern Hemisphere. Even if one had, by some miracle, brought about an agreement to abolish nuclear weapons, or had established an European nuclear-free zone, the wide knowledge of how to construct them would soon lead to their reappearance if conventional hostilities lasted for any length of time.

There are others who say that wars never achieve anything, and that conflicts of interest and ideas should and can be resolved without resort to violence of any kind; if we set an example in that respect, others will follow. They generally base their case on the injunction in the Sermon on the Mount: 'whosoever shall smite thee on thy right cheek turn to him the other also', but those who quote it seldom stress the words that precede it—'Resist not evil'.[1] The sad fact—and all history and one's own experience bear it out—is that if one does not resist evil, it will prevail. If the evil man, intent on pursuing his own interests, whatever the motive, forces his way on others by violence or by intimidating them with the threat of violence, and is not resisted, if necessary by force, he will prevail.

It is true that many wars seem to have been in vain, not to have furthered the policies of which they have been a continuation, but much depends on the point of view from which one regards them. Many of the nations of the world today, certainly the larger ones, have resulted from wars that brought them into existence—France and Britain a long time ago; the United States as a result both of her War of Independence against Britain and her own Civil War; Germany, Italy and Russia as a result of war in the nineteenth century. Many smaller countries have gained their independence by resort to war, Zimbabwe being one of the most recent to do so. If one were to ask Americans if the Vietnam war had achieved its aim, they would say 'No,' but Giap and the late Ho Chi-minh would answer 'Yes'. Whether the inhabitants of the countries involved are any better off as a result is another question, although admittedly a relevant one. Israel would not exist if the Jews had not fought Britain in order to establish their right to a country of their own, and then the Arabs to secure it. They would emphatically say that their wars had been effective, whereas the Arab countries, who fought against them, could only truthfully admit that, from their point of view, they had not.

Clausewitz's dilemma remains. The conduct of the war, and its after-effects, can cause such destruction, suffering and turmoil that, even though in the end you may have defeated the enemy's armed forces and imposed your will on him, you are no better off, perhaps even worse off, than you

---

[1] Matthew 5:39.

were when you started. The First World War must surely fall into that category. What about the Second? How do casualties, the suffering and destruction, the fate that many peoples suffered as an indirect result, weigh in the balance against the removal of the canker of Hitler's political and racial creed from Europe? What would Europe and the world be like today if the Nazi and Japanese forms of totalitarian tyranny had not been resisted and defeated? The answer that history gives is that war *can* be an effective continuation of policy—certainly this is so if it is waged in resistance to one who is himself using or threatening violence to gain his ends—but its effectiveness depends on how it is conducted. The sooner it is brought to a conclusion the better. That may well involve using a high, rather than a low, degree of force. The test must be whether a continuation of the war is going to achieve the policy of which it is itself a continuation. The unilateral Chinese decision in 1962 to halt and withdraw, as soon as they had achieved their aim of teaching India a lesson over their frontier war, was an admirable example of this.

If war, in certain circumstances, is effective in achieving the aim of a policy, when persuasion or economic pressure has failed to achieve it, is it nevertheless acceptable to kill people, and to cause suffering and damage to many more, in order to do so? Were the Jews justified in fighting for a land of their own? Are the Palestinians justified in fighting to get it back? Were Mugabe and Nkomo justified not only in killing Rhodesians, black and white, but in imposing great misery and hardship on most of their fellow blacks who were caught in the crossfire? Are the inhabitants of Vietnam, Laos and Cambodia better off because Ho Chi-minh fought to get rid of the French and impose Communism on the area? Or the Algerians as a result of their long and bitter struggle with the French? There are no straightforward answers to these questions. They depend on the point of view one starts from, and the importance one attaches to different things. Which is more important: freedom to run one's own affairs, or a material standard of living? Does the preservation of human life take priority over everything else, whatever the conditions in which it is preserved?

The pursuit of justice for one's own group, which may involve political change, will almost certainly come into conflict with the demand for peace, just as the maintenance of peace may involve the continuation of injustice; and justice for some may involve injustice for others. There are no easy, black-and-white solutions. We must seek a policy that achieves the best possible balance between peace and justice, between stability and change.

At the heart of the problem is the need to recognize that two fundamentally opposed concepts of how society should be organized have to learn to live in peace together, at least for the present and the foreseeable future. Two highly intelligent Americans, who have viewed the problem from rather different angles, have aired somewhat similar views about this. One is George Kennan, who wrote in a recent article:

> This tendency to view all aspects of the relationship in terms of a supposed total and irreconcilable conflict of concern and aims: these are not the marks of the maturity and discrimination one expects of the diplomacy of a great power; they are the marks of an intellectual primitivism and naiveté unpardonable in a great government. I use the word naiveté, because there is a naiveté of cynicism and suspicion just as there is a naiveté of innocence.
>
> And we shall not be able to turn these things around as they should be turned, on the plane of military and nuclear rivalry, until we learn to correct these childish distortions—until we correct our tendency to see in the Soviet Union only a mirror in which we look for the reflection of our own virtue—until we consent to see there another great people, one of the world's greatest, in all its complexity and variety, embracing the good with the bad—a people whose life, whose views, whose habits,

> whose fears and aspirations, whose successes and failures, are the products, just as ours are the products, not of any inherent iniquity but of the relentless discipline of history, tradition and national experience. Above all, we must learn to see the behavior of the leadership of that country as partly the reflection of our own treatment of it. If we insist on demonizing these Soviet leaders—on viewing them as total and incorrigible enemies, consumed only with their fear or hatred of us and dedicated to nothing other than our destruction—that, in the end, is the way we shall assuredly have them—if for no other reason than that our view of them allows for nothing else—either for them or for us.[1]

The other was Henry Kissinger, who wrote this:

> How to avoid nuclear war without succumbing to nuclear blackmail, how to prevent the desire for peace from turning into appeasement; how to defend liberty and maintain the peace—this is the overwhelming problem of our age. . . . Confrontations not perceived as necessary by the public will divide each country, split our alliances, and produce a quest for peace at any price. No self-respecting democratic leader can sustain himself by treating vigilance and peace as if they were opposites. Our alliances will be sundered if they appear to be obstacles to peace. To be sure, détente is dangerous if it does not include a strategy of containment. But containment is unsustainable unless coupled with a notion of peace. The remedy is not to evade the effort to define coexistence; it is to give it a content that reflects our principles and our objectives.[2]

Our hope must be that the contradictions inherent in their organization of society will eventually force a

---

[1] 'On Nuclear War', *New York Review of Books*, 21 January 1982.
[2] 'How to Deal With Moscow in a Nuclear Age,' *The Times*, 24 February 1982.

transformation from within, just as similar contradictions inherent in the policy of apartheid are beginning to undermine the system in South Africa.

But that does not mean that we can let down our guard. The Soviet Union is an immensely powerful military nation and would undoubtedly use that power to further her political ends, if she could do so with impunity. 'Peaceful coexistence' does not mean that the struggle for world influence and power will cease. It was defined by Herr Ulbricht of East Germany as

> a particular form of struggle by the forces of socialism with imperialism in the international arena. The purpose is to obtain maximum results for socialism in the process of competition, by means of skilful politics by the communist and workers' parties under the leadership of the Soviet Union, without giving the capitalists apparent reason to use armed forces.[1]

But Brezhnev did not rule out the use of armed force in this struggle. In Prague in 1968 he said: 'If we want to win we cannot achieve our goals without strong military forces. Did we ever say that we would not use force if it was necessary to support progressive movements in, for example, France, Britain or Sweden? This is the sacred duty of our forces—to protect and support progressive movements.' We must be prepared to meet the threat of force with force: we must not allow ourselves to be intimidated.

If we are to be prepared to defend ourselves, must we rely on the threat of nuclear weapons, or are there other methods of defence to which we could turn, allowing us, that is, NATO, to discard such weapons and work towards their total abolition? A number of 'alternative strategies' have been proposed, some of them associated with the policy of disengaging the great powers from Europe west of Russia, which has already been discussed. One is that the nations of

---

[1] Speech, December 1968.

Western Europe, including Britain, should rely on passive civil resistance, a policy of non-violent non-co-operation. Examples are quoted of the success of such policies in India against Britain, in many of the nations within both the Austro–Hungarian and Ottoman Empires, and in Norway against the German occupation in the Second World War. But although such resistance succeeded in preserving the national identity of the peoples concerned, in no case did it force the occupying authority to withdraw, even, in some cases, after centuries of occupation. Others favour resort to guerrilla or partisan warfare. Similar criticism can be levelled against that; in addition it causes great misery to the inhabitants of the country who find themselves ground between the upper and the nether millstones of the occupying power and the partisans. Thomas Arnold in 1842 made this apt comment on it:

> The truth is that if war, carried out by regular armies under the strictest discipline, is yet a great evil, an irregular partisan warfare is an evil ten times more intolerable; it is in fact to give licence to a whole population to commit all sorts of treachery, rapine and cruelty, without any restraint; letting loose a multitude of armed men, with none of the obedience and none of the honourable feelings of the soldier.

A variant of this alternative strategy is to rely on a widespread network of territorial or local defence, based on small bodies of men defending their local area, a type of Home Guard. But in this case they would be uniformed and would observe the recognized laws and usages of war, rather than the 'no holds barred' tactics of guerrilla or partisan forces.

The prospect of having to deal with these forms of defence is not likely to deter a country like the Soviet Union, which has massive military resources, not least of manpower, and is insensitive to both domestic and international opinion about how they are used. Nor would such strategies provide forces that could quickly seal off and contain an invasion which had a limited aim or had resulted from some misunderstanding, an eventuality that is more likely than that of a massive all-out invasion designed to overrun the whole of Europe. None of these strategies would provide any defence against air attack, except by slow, low-flying aircraft.

Others suggest, as McNamara did and, at times, Kissinger, that the countries of Western Europe should provide sufficient purely conventional forces to provide an adequate conventional defence. There is no doubt that they have the manpower and the industrial resources to be able to do this, if they were determined to. Others, while accepting that NATO should continue to rely on American nuclear power to deter war, suggest that we in Britain should follow the Scandinavian lead and refuse to have nuclear weapons and their delivery systems based on our soil, in the hope that this would prevent us from being a target for Soviet nuclear attack. Apart from its effect on the cohesion of NATO, this seems to me to be hypocritical. If NATO relies on nuclear deterrence, and if it is considered to be a necessary part of NATO's strategy that there should be land-based delivery systems in Europe, we must be prepared, together with our fellow European allies, to take our share of the risks. Excluded from Britain, where is it proposed that those systems should go? Germany bears her full share already, France excludes any but her own, and the Low Countries would not show any enthusiasm to receive them. Others propose a European Nuclear-Free Zone, some from the Atlantic to the Urals, others from the Atlantic to the Russian frontier. Even the former would not necessarily spare Europe from the effects of a nuclear war, as delivery systems based outside the area, on land or at sea, could still deliver warheads onto targets within it by missiles or aircraft.

It cannot be denied that the concept of nuclear deterrence abounds in illogicalities and paradoxes. At the heart of the problem is the dilemma that if one wishes to deter war by the fear that nuclear weapons will be used, one has to appear to be prepared to use them in certain circumstances. But if one does so, and the enemy answers back, as he has the capability to do and has clearly said he would, one is very much worse off than if one had not done so, if indeed one is there at all. To pose an unacceptable risk to the enemy automatically poses the same risk to oneself. But to attempt to reduce the risk in order to make the threat more credible—through some form of limited nuclear war, territorially, or by types of target or means of delivery—begins to make that risk more acceptable and therefore less of a deterrent. The more acceptable nuclear war may appear to be to the governments and military men of the nuclear powers, the more likely it is that it will actually come about and, even if it is limited in some way, the effects on those who live in the countries, in or over which the nuclear weapons of both sides are exploded, will be catastrophic. To call the results defence or security makes a mockery of the terms.

Ever since the two giant nuclear powers achieved the capability for mutual assured destruction (MAD), the best strategic brains have been trying to escape from this dilemma by inventing various concepts of limited nuclear use, most of which have been described in previous chapters. They vary from counterforce strategies, through limited use of both strategic and theatre systems, to Beaufre's 'sublimited' nuclear war. All fail on four grounds.

First, there can never be a guarantee that the nuclear exchange will remain limited to the extent that the initiator hopes—indeed, it is inherent in deterrent strategy that in the last of last resorts it should not. Second, there is no guarantee that the initiator will come out better off as a result of the exchange. In fact, the probability in both cases is that if the West were the initiator, the exchange would not be as limited as is hoped, and that even if it were, the West would come off worst, the result partly of geography, partly of the overall balance of conventional forces. This is the reason why Gavin, Beaufre and others pointed out that if one wished one's armed forces to survive a nuclear war, one needed larger, not smaller, ones. The only case in which this would not be the outcome would be if the enemy's riposte were even more limited or perhaps not nuclear at all. Supporters of this concept argue that if the Soviet Union were to invade Western Europe, it would be because she wished to occupy it and acquire its resources. She would not therefore wish to damage it. To initiate a nuclear exchange on that assumption would be criminally irresponsible. The reason for Soviet aggression is more likely to be to prevent the West from interfering in affairs east of the Iron Curtain.

The third ground of objection to limited nuclear use is that it undermines the fundamental basis of nuclear deterrence, which is to pose an unacceptable risk. The fourth is that public support for such a policy is difficult to enlist.

Faced with these paradoxes, strategists take refuge in distinguishing what they threaten to do from what they would actually do in the event, which helps those who are familiar with moral casuistry to salve their consciences. But few things are more dangerous in confrontations that involve conflict than to threaten some action which one does not intend in the event to implement; when one's bluff is called, one has either to climb down or to do something that one had decided before-hand it was unwise to do. Such a stance opens up a wide 'credibility gap', which undermines the value of deterrence. Beaufre was guilty of this when, searching for 'first-strike credibility' and having been forced by his clear and logical mind to discard all other forms of limited war or use, he disregarded the factors listed above and fell back on the assertion that, because his proposed 'sublimited' nuclear war was the only way of making a first strike appear credible, 'it must therefore be considered feasible.' In other words: it will not work, but if I go on saying so loud enough and long enough, people will believe that it will.

The stark truth is that all that the huge nuclear arsenals of the United States and the Soviet Union now do is deter them both from fighting each other and, if that were tragically to fail, deter them both from using nuclear weapons against each other. They cannot be stretched to deter anything else, because the search for nuclear superiority, which is essential for such an extension, has been proved to be in vain. In spite of all the disadvantages, which Kissinger, Beaufre and others have recognized, that stem from a stable nuclear balance, it is in the interests of the whole world that it should be preserved. Even though its deterrent value is limited, prevention of war between the two world powers, whose concepts of how to organize human society are so diametrically opposed, is a very significant and valuable contribution to world peace, for which we should be grateful. Those who wish to abolish nuclear weapons altogether, who say that we are 'on the brink of the final abyss', who predict that nuclear war within the next decade is inevitable, disregard this factor tending to stability and are guilty of panic-mongering. As Beaufre wrote:

> Peace is far more stable than before the advent of the nuclear weapon. But peace has no longer the absolute character it had in the last century: today it is possible to hurl insults at a nation, burn down its embassy, arrest its ships, send hired assassins into its country or give almost open support to political parties without war breaking out; formerly this would have been unthinkable. Peace between contending nations has become 'war in peacetime' or cold war.[1]

Abolition of nuclear weapons would turn the clock back to the era in which the major industrial nations could think

---

[1] *Deterrence and Strategy*, pp. 29–30.

of war as an acceptable 'other means' of continuing policy. The results of that in the twentieth century have been bad enough, and a major war with modern conventional weapons would be far more destructive than that of 1939–45. But we should not be putting the clock back entirely, because the knowledge of how to make a nuclear weapon is now widespread, and the means of doing so more easily come by than in 1945. By abolishing, or appearing to abolish, nuclear weapons, we should be making a Third World War more likely, and, if it started as a conventional one and lasted any length of time, there is no doubt that the nuclear weapon would reappear. We would then have the worst of both worlds. We would have lost its value as a deterrent but would suffer from its use after the war had started. The sure foundation of our policy must therefore be the continuation of the mutual nuclear deterrent to war in the hands of the giant powers. That can be extended to cover the security of Europe—and other areas—not by attempts to achieve nuclear superiority nor by proliferation in the numbers of nations that possess them, but by the clear commitment, on the one hand, of the United States to the defence of the free world, and, on the other, of the Soviet Union to her own Communist bloc. In the case of Europe, that is guaranteed by the presence of the conventional forces of each to the areas west and east of the Iron Curtain respectively. If either the United States were not committed to the West or the Soviet Union to the East, or neither to either, a very unstable situation would be created, in which some nation, or part of one, might be tempted to juggle the kaleidoscope of frontiers, and off Europe would go again down the sad road of internecine warfare from which it has suffered so grievously down the centuries.

The deterrent to war is therefore both nuclear and conventional. To insist that the nuclear deterrent must remain an essential element is not to say that the vast arsenals on both sides are necessary to maintain a stable balance. They have been brought about very largely by the search for superiority and for forms of limited nuclear use. Once it is accepted that those are vain objectives, a large part of the arsenal is seen to be superfluous, particularly that deriving from concepts of fighting a limited nuclear war (for instance, artillery shells and most of the bombs intended to be delivered by aircraft). An invulnerable retaliatory force, capable of a certain degree of 'assured destruction', is all that is needed for a strategic force. It is the vulnerability of land-based systems that has led to the great race in the strategic field.

The question remains as to whether it is necessary to base some systems in Europe, and specifically on land in Europe, in order to reassure the Europeans that their security is linked to that of America, and to discourage the Soviet Union from thinking that she could employ nuclear weapons herself in Europe without risk of retaliation. For NATO's conventional forces to have no nuclear backing other than American strategic systems, while the Soviet Union had nuclear weapons clearly designed for use against Europe, would be to run an unjustifiable risk. But, as with strategic systems, the need is not for an exact balance in the numbers of warheads one can deliver, but for a force that can deliver an attack which makes the risk unacceptably high. In both the strategic and the theatre fields, therefore, we should aim for a reduction in systems to such a level. Arms control negotiations invariably become bogged down in discussions of numbers and methods of verifying them. They should aim rather at agreements not to employ certain systems, such as artillery and certain types of aircraft. The systems that remain should, as far as possible, be ones that are invulnerable—as a result of mobility on land, at sea, or even in the air—and against which there is little probability of providing an adequate defence: ballistic missiles are therefore to be preferred. These two characteristics will discourage competition to produce a counterforce and a defence, and also a first strike to pre-empt or prevent their use. They will therefore aid stability in the balance.

Recognition that limited nuclear war has no part to play in our strategy inevitably means that greater emphasis must be placed on conventional forces, both to deter war and, if that were to fail, to control and, one hopes, restore the situation. The nuclear shadow hanging over all will be a strong influence on the side of restraint, as the Cuban crisis showed. It is very difficult to imagine a conventional war, involving the forces of the United States and of the Soviet Union, continuing for long under that shadow. The longer it went on, the greater would be the temptation to raise the stakes, either on the side that appeared to be losing or on the side that had hoped for a swift victory and was disappointed. The most likely origin of war in Europe, on the assumption that both the giants still maintain their forces on either side of the Iron Curtain, is of some instability within Eastern Europe or on its frontiers, in which one side or the other fears direct intervention by the other. Tension could lead to preparatory military measures being taken, to which both would react on the pattern of 1914. As at that time, each side would fear that the other would establish an advantage in preparedness, which would give it a decisive advantage if hostilities broke out—a self-fulfilling process. That is surely more likely than the 'bolt from the blue' or the massive premeditated sweep across Europe that NATO planners tend to envisage and try to prepare for.

Ever since the earliest days of NATO, when the politicians were faced by the 'Lisbon goal' of ninety divisions, they have rejected the demands of the military planners as imposing impossibly unrealistic burdens both on finance and on the length of conscript service needed to produce the manpower. For some years they tried to pull the wool over their own eyes by planning to produce 'post-M Day' (Mobilization Day) divisions, formed from reservists, most of whom were ex-conscripts who had done no training since they had finished their service. The only equipment available was dwindling stocks of wartime material. When that ran out, the divisions became even more mythical than they had been. In any case, by that stage the idea that there would be time to form, train and move such divisions to the battlefield had evaporated. Instant 'combat readiness' was the order of the day.

Unless NATO is given a severe fright, worse than those of the Berlin crises, it is clear that the European members are not going to be prepared to devote to defence the much greater resources of money and manpower that would be needed to add significantly to its standing forces. As it is, keeping them up to date in equipment absorbs more than the 3 per cent increase in real terms which they have undertaken to provide. The answer must lie in a new and radical look at the possibility of improving the conventional capability by a better use of reserve manpower. At present, the ex-conscripts of Continental countries and ex-regulars of Britain are called up on mobilization to fill gaps in the ranks of units of the standing forces, where they provide much of the logistical and administrative backing, and, in the case of Britain, by volunteers of the Territorial Army, to provide additional combat units, with less modern equipment than that of the standing forces, generally for use in a secondary combat role. The West German Territorial Army, the permanent staff of which in peace numbers 40,000, is brought to a strength of 480,000 with reservists on mobilization, equal to the strength of the standing army. Of this personnel, 11 per cent are allocated to logistic units, 16 per cent to medical, and 27 per cent as reinforcements to replace casualties in the whole army. The remaining 46 per cent are allocated to combat duties, a large proportion to 'home defence brigades'. This large army is under national, not NATO, command and has only a loose form of liaison with allied contingents operating in Germany. It seldom features in NATO's calculations. Soviet and other Warsaw Pact forces today are primarily armoured: tanks, infantry in armoured personnel carriers and self-propelled artillery. To stop them, rifles and machine-guns are not enough: anti-armour weapons are required. Fortunately such weapons can now be produced that do not depend upon kinetic energy to penetrate armour, and therefore do not need heavy vehicles to move them. For the shorter ranges, manportable weapons, capable of penetrating the thickest armour, can now be made available in quantity. They are not cheap, nothing is cheap, but they are very good value for money, and the operator does not need complicated and expensive training.

A reorganization of the reserves to provide a large number of anti-armour units, supplemented by volunteers or older ex-conscripts, raised on a local, territorial basis, similar to the Danish Home Guard, could significantly improve the capability of NATO's conventional forces. They could, perhaps, assume responsibility for the static framework of defence, including the laying and guarding of minefields, allowing the standing forces, both German and Allied, to act as a mobile reserve. An essential element in such a structure would be that the Territorial forces were fully integrated into the overall NATO command system. The same pattern should be extended to other NATO countries—in fact it exists in certain forms in some of them. In Britain, it could be applied to Home Defence, although the threat of direct attack by land forces is a remote one, unless NATO had totally failed in its task of defending Western Europe. This could free more Territorial Army units to reinforce the British army in Germany.

The urgent need is for NATO to abandon the concept that it can avert conventional defeat by initiating nuclear war: it would only result in an even greater defeat. Its military men must stop training their soldiers, airmen and sailors to make that assumption. Its politicians and officials must stop thinking that the existence of nuclear weapons of any kind means that they can economize on conventional forces. Both must give the latter first priority, and concentrate their attention and resources on methods of improving their capability. This will mean that the nuclear deterrent to war will be strengthened and that, if it were to fail, the risk of events slipping inevitably into the horror of a nuclear exchange will be greatly reduced.

With such a policy, is there any reason for Britain to have her own nuclear weapons and, in particular, to maintain an independent strategic deterrent force? The arguments about independent forces have already been discussed. There can be no doubt that there is no need to add to the number of nuclear weapons that the United States already deploys in Europe. Far from it—as has been suggested, the need is to reduce them. If the argument for it is basically a polite version of the 'Trigger Argument'—the second centre of decision—that is irrelevant if one believes that it would be folly to initiate nuclear war in Europe, and that to threaten it opens up a credibility gap between threats and intentions. If the basic motive is that it is an insurance against American abandonment of Europe and a subsequent collapse of NATO, all the arguments that Kissinger, Beaufre and others used against a minor nuclear power threatening a major nuclear power, describing it as 'tantamount to suicide', are relevant. If it is that a Western European military alliance of some kind could survive without the Americans, relying on the nuclear deterrent forces of Britain and France, the same arguments apply. The overriding importance of the presence of United States forces in Europe has already been argued. If the concept of an alliance without the Americans is valid, no harm could supposedly result from their departure now.

Another justification is that it would preserve Britain from nuclear attack, either in the context of a nuclear exchange within NATO, or if NATO had collapsed and Britain stood alone. If a nuclear exchange had occurred involving the USA and the USSR, the fact that Britain had a force of her own (which it must be assumed had not yet fired its weapons in support of NATO) is unlikely to deter the Soviet Union from attacking nuclear delivery systems in Europe, wherever they may be. She would risk much greater retaliation from the American nuclear forces than she would from the British. In the second context, it would, as has been already been argued, be 'tantamount to suicide' to threaten their use. In both contexts, the diametrically opposed argument can be used: that it is the existence of bases for nuclear delivery systems in Britain that invites attack.

If the arguments that have been expounded in this and earlier chapters are accepted, there can be no doubt that to spend a considerable sum on replacing Britain's four Polaris-equipped submarines by four or five Trident-equipped ones, which would significantly increase the number of warheads, represents a fundamentally wrong allocation of priorities in defence. Whatever the purely military balance of advantage, one argument against Britain giving up her own independent deterrent, which applies also to giving up her own nuclear weapons altogether, is that it would lower her status as a nation, particularly in relation to France. The latter claims that her independent strategic nuclear force is the foundation of her ability to pursue an independent policy. Britain has learnt the sad lesson that it is not possible in the world today for any nation to pursue an independent policy, least of all one of which the economic basis is shaky. France's independence in policy is more imaginary then real. Status, like power to a degree, is what one thinks it is. In that respect France's independent nuclear status has helped her to regain her self-respect and self-confidence, shattered by the humiliations of Indo-China and Algeria, following on that of 1940, with memories of 1870 still lingering on. It has been a useful, perhaps invaluable political asset, which has united rather than divided the nation. Its value as a symbol of independence will probably fade with time. Britain's independent deterrent does not serve the same purpose, although it was intended to by the government that created it and those who have made the decisions to preserve it. The policy of successive British governments, of both colours, apart from the aberration of Suez, has been based on the closest possible Anglo-American co-operation, supplemented more recently by European co-operation. Attempts to pursue independent policies have not proved fruitful. Britain does not need an independent strategic force for that political purpose, and it divides rather than unites the nation. Ironically, it is the political party that is opposed to an independent strategic force that tends to advocate pursuit of a policy independent both of the United States and of Europe. It is the party that, logically, should favour such a force.

If Britain does not replace her Polaris SLBM force, should she continue to possess her own nuclear warheads and man delivery systems? The highest priority in Britain's defence is the cohesion of NATO, the keystone of which is the continued support of the United States. As long as NATO decides that it must have some nuclear delivery systems based in Europe or in its surrounding waters, we should take our share of manning the appropriate delivery systems. But the numbers of these systems should be reduced, and it should be our aim to encourage the Americans to enlarge the Geneva talks on theatre systems to embrace all 'forward-based systems', as the Russians have demanded, including our own systems, both submarine-launched and aircraft-delivered. If, in the course of those negotiations, it would assist progress for us to give up producing and possessing our own warheads, we should be prepared to do so. The reasons for having our own are political rather than military, and a significant sum could be saved if we abandoned the capability to design, manufacture and maintain them. As long as we continue to have our own warheads, even if we never design another, we have to maintain that capability. We should also suggest to NATO that the abolition of nuclear weapons for artillery and for shorter-range aircraft of the fighter bomber type should be proposed in those negotiations. In all these matters, we must take the lead in NATO, but not act alone, which could seriously affect the cohesion of the alliance.

Apart from the political arguments for keeping one's own weapons, there are those who say that one cannot forecast the future and safely assume that the present international structure will always remain. In an uncertain world, in which proliferation has perhaps increased, Britain could find herself in conflict with a minor nuclear power, when not supported by a major one. If the world evolved in a way that made that likely, and it was thought that having one's own nuclear weapons was essential to the nation's security in it, Britain would already have the knowledge and, with nuclear power stations, some of the essential capability to get back into the business if she wanted to, in a much shorter period than it took her to create the capability in the 1950s.

Finally, we should place greater emphasis on the development of confidence-building measures. A thin end of a promising wedge was inserted at Helsinki in this direction, and the French have made further valuable proposals at the Madrid follow-up conference. Mutually tolerated satellite photography has been the greatest confidence-building measure of all. It significantly reduces the potential area of misunderstanding and the exaggerated fears that are so apt to bedevil relations between East and West and that lead to tension and encourage an arms race. Realistic and mutually acceptable confidence-building measures could do much to encourage a feeling of mutual trust, without which agreements on arms control, nuclear or conventional, cannot be obtained. The aim of arms control must be to achieve and maintain a stable balance of strength. Weakness invites instability. In the search for peace, it must not be overlooked that the higher the risks of war, the less likely it is that statesmen will embark upon it. Attempts to reduce the horrors of war, or the burden of providing armed forces, tend to make war appear more acceptable, and it therefore becomes more likely. And once it starts, all the experience of history goes to show that it is extremely difficult to limit or to stop it. There is truth in the maxim of

Vegetius: 'Let him who desires peace, prepare for war', but Liddell Hart was right to add that it was above all important that he who desired peace should *understand* war. Such understanding involves an intellectual effort which, unfortunately, few military men, and even fewer politicians, are prepared to make. Peace will not be preserved by adherence to outworn concepts, unrelated to realities and based on emotion. This applies both to the hawks and to the doves.

En fin du compte, as the French say, we face a terrible dilemma. The existence of nuclear weapons on both sides of the great ideological divide restrains armed conflict. But, if that restraint were to fail, it could, not necessarily would, mean the obliteration of civilization and terrible consequences for all forms of life. The first challenge is to plot a course that exploits one with the least risk of the other; the second is to persuade our own nation, our fellow members of NATO and the Western (indeed the whole) world that it is the right course to follow; and the third challenge is to have the resolution to persist in it.

Index